---

35 INSPIRING WAYS TO BE A SUCCESSFUL AUTHOR

The Positive Writer's Mindset

S. A. SOULE

FWT PRESS

Contents

Preface

FWT Press appreciates its readers, and every effort has been made to properly edit this guidebook. However, typos and misspellings and grammar mistakes are occasionally overlooked. If you find an error in the text, please send us an email so the issue can be corrected. Thank you!

Please do not upload this book anywhere for free. That is pirating, and stealing is not cool. Not that you, dear reader, would ever do anything illegal, because you are just too awesome.

Introduction

Dear Future Successful Author,

I remember when I first began my writing career. It was a blend of excitement that I was following my dreams, my purpose, and absolute terror. My fingers trembled over the keyboard, unsure if the words I typed would ever resonate with anyone. But I pushed through, driven by an insatiable desire to tell the stories that I wanted to write.

In this book, we can define what success looks like for you and your writing career, whether you're a ghostwriter, an aspiring writer, or a seasoned author. Success isn't a one-size-fits-all concept; it's as unique as the stories we craft. And while some topics might seem repetitive, if you're like me, you might need to hear (or in this case, read) something more than once before it really sinks in.

When it comes to becoming a successful author, there are countless paths to take. But through the principles of the law of attraction, I've discovered approaches that have worked wonders for me and many others. The goal of this book is to offer you those tools, tips, and strategies so that you, too, can create a fulfilling and successful writing career. Plus, I'll share anecdotes from my own life as an author and a few from other writers, hoping they'll inspire and motivate you.

To be honest, when I first discovered the law of attraction, I was skeptical. It sounded too good to be true—just think positively and success will follow?

As I began to apply its principles, I noticed subtle shifts. Opportunities seemed to appear out of nowhere; connections were made effortlessly, and money flowed to me. Then I realized that our mindset plays a crucial role in shaping our reality.

For over ten years, I've studied the law of attraction, manifesting countless amazing things in my life. This book is my way of sharing how you too can manifest your dreams and achieve success. Writing has been a passion of mine for most of my life.

This business isn't just about accumulating accolades or hitting bestseller lists—though those milestones are awesome. It's about aligning yourself with your deepest desires and allowing those dreams to come to fruition. It's about thriving in creativity and authenticity.

Every step of my career has taught me something invaluable. Whether it was the late nights editing manuscripts until my eyes blurred or the exhilarating moment of seeing my name on a bestseller list, each experience has added to my understanding of what it takes to succeed as an author. And now, I'm excited to share those insights with you.

In this book, you'll find advice on becoming more positive, focused, and motivated, with inspiring ways to accomplish your dreams. My aim is to provide you with the means to support your vision, and become the author you aspire to be.

Now let me tell you a bit about myself and why I wanted to write this guidebook. I've been working in the publishing world for over fifteen years, as a developmental editor, ghostwriter, author, and book cover designer. I majored in Creative Writing in college and even owned an eBook publishing company. After that, I worked as an acquisition editor for another publisher. In the past five years, I've had the privilege of editing books for several bestselling authors.

Also, I've written fifteen fiction novels under various pen names and ten nonfiction titles. Many of my books have made it to the Kindle Top 100 bestseller lists, and some of my fiction has been selected as top picks on several prominent review sites. So, I've had some moderate success, and it was the law of attraction that changed my life and my career.

Writing is an art, but it's also a craft that requires dedication and resilience. It's about finding joy in the process, and reaping the rewards of the end result.

Imagine waking up each morning energized and excited about your writing. Visualize yourself sitting down at your desk, words flowing effortlessly because you're aligned with your purpose and passion. Feel the joy of holding your published book in your hands, knowing it's a product of your hard work and dedication.

Throughout this book, I'll reveal techniques for harnessing the power of the law of attraction to draw success and inspiration into your life. These aren't just abstract concepts—they're practical steps I've used, and they can work for you too.

Becoming a successful author is not a sprint—it's a marathon. It requires patience, perseverance, and a willingness to welcome both the highs and the lows. But with the right mindset, you can turn your dreams into your truth.

In the chapters ahead, we'll explore positive approaches and more, providing you with actionable steps to integrate them into your routine. You'll learn how to set intentions, visualize success, and maintain a positive outlook even when faced with challenges.

While this guide is only my personal opinion on this topic, there are many ways to be a successful author. I encourage you to take all of these suggestions to heart and only make the changes in your life and career that you feel best match your goals.

This guide is definitely not a "grammar do or don't," because honestly, mine is not the best. However, my goal is always for writers to come away with a positive mindset that helps them achieve the success that they deserve.

Are you ready to level up your career?

Let's explore the power of positivity, the magic of the law of attraction, and the practical steps you can take to turn your writing dreams into your new reality.

Let's get started!

35 INSPIRING WAYS TO BE A SUCCESSFUL AUTHOR

Successful Author Mindset

THE LAW of attraction states that what you think about, you bring about. So why not start thinking and acting like a successful author, right now? By adopting the mindset and habits of a bestselling writer, you align yourself with the success you aspire to achieve. Let's explore how to embody the author boss you are destined to be.

The Power of Acting As If

Acting as if you're already a successful author means making choices and behaving in ways that reflect your desired reality. It's about having the mindset of a positive, bestselling author and making decisions that support your vision.

By stepping into this mindset, you start to create routines and habits that mimic those of successful authors. This might mean setting a daily writing schedule, engaging with your readers regularly, or investing time in learning more about the current publishing trends. When you act as if you're already living your dream, you're not just playing a role—you're actively shifting your reality to align with your goals. This mental shift opens you up to new opportunities and draws the success you seek closer, making the dream of becoming a bestselling author a tangible and attainable reality.

Also, I suggest making choices like a successful author, which means being strategic and professional in all aspects of your career. This includes your online presence. Always present yourself in a manner that reflects your best self. Share content that resonates with your brand and engages your audience, while avoiding unnecessary negativity or unprofessional behavior. Interact with your readers and fellow authors in a respectful and encouraging manner. By maintaining a professional demeanor online and making choices that reflect the level of success you aspire to, you'll build a reputation that attracts more readers, opportunities, and ultimately, success. Here are some ways you can have a successful mindset.

Successful Author Mindset Tips:

- Visualize Your Success: Spend a few minutes each day visualizing your ultimate goals. Imagine yourself at book signings, receiving positive reviews, and celebrating your books hitting bestseller lists. The more vividly you can picture your success, the more real it becomes in your mind.

- Set Clear Intentions: Write down specific goals you want to achieve as an author. Whether it's finishing a manuscript, landing a publishing deal, or growing your readership, having clear intentions helps direct your focus and energy.

- Positive Affirmations: Use positive affirmations to reinforce your belief in your success. Statements like "I am a successful author" or "My words inspire and captivate readers" can help shift your mindset towards achieving your goals.

- Practice Gratitude: Begin each day by listing things you are grateful for. Gratitude shifts your focus from what you lack to the abundance you already have, attracting more positive experiences into your life.

- Surround Yourself with Positivity: Engage with supportive and like-minded individuals. Join writing groups, attend workshops, and network with other authors who inspire and uplift you.

- Take Inspired Action: The law of attraction emphasizes the power of mindset, but it also requires action. Take concrete steps towards your goals, no matter how minor. Action amplifies your intentions and brings you closer to your dreams.

- Maintain a Growth Mindset: Embrace challenges and learn from failures. Viewing obstacles as opportunities for growth keeps you resilient and enthusiastic to accomplish your dreams.

- Stay Persistent and Patient: Success doesn't happen overnight. Keep your focus and remain patient, trusting that your efforts will pay off in due time.

- Eliminate Negative Self-Talk: Be mindful of your inner dialogue. Replace negative thoughts with positive ones. Instead of thinking, "I'll never finish this book," tell yourself, "I am making steady progress every day."

- Focus on a Vision Board: Look at your board with the images and words that represent your goals and dreams. Place it where you can see it daily to keep your focus on your aspirations.

- Act As If You Are Already Successful: Make choices and behave in ways that reflect your desired reality. Treat your writing career with the professionalism and dedication it deserves.

- Align Your Environment: Ensure your workspace and surroundings reflect your goals. A tidy, inspiring space can significantly impact your productivity and creativity.

By incorporating these tips into your daily routine, you cultivate a mindset that aligns with your aspirations, attracting success and opportunities that bring your dreams to life.

Acting the Part of a Successful Author

As a single mom with four cats and an insatiable coffee habit, life can get pretty chaotic. But I realized that if I wanted to be a successful author, I needed to start acting like one.

One day, I decided to make some changes. First, I revamped my writing space. Gone were the piles of laundry and half-eaten bags of cat treats (courtesy of my mischievous felines). Instead, I created a cozy, cat-friendly nook with a desk, a comfy chair, and shelves lined with my favorite books. My four furry muses—Sushi, Boujee, Jinx, and Kuromi—approved of the new setup immediately.

Next, I started dressing the part. Now, I'm not saying I wore evening gowns to my writing sessions, but I did trade in my worn-out sweatpants for something a bit more polished. There's something about putting on nice, comfy pajamas that makes you feel like you've got your life together.

I also set clear, ambitious goals. One of my objectives was to finish my novel within three months. I broke this down into weekly word count targets and did little happy dances in my PJs each time I hit my word count with an extra cup of coffee (and maybe a cat cuddle or two).

My mornings transformed into a ritual of success. I'd start with a bit of meditation to clear my mind, followed by jotting down my daily goals and affirmations in a journal. This practice grounded me, helping me approach my writing with clarity and intention. I found that by dedicating the first hour of my day to these positive habits, my productivity leveled up, and my focus sharpened. It was as if the Universe took note of my dedication and began aligning events and opportunities in my favor.

Through this practice, I learned that the law of attraction isn't just about thinking positively—it's about embodying the success you seek. By making choices that reflected my desired reality, I aligned myself with opportunities and achievements that might have otherwise seemed out of reach.

Now start acting like the successful author you are destined to be. Dress the part, create an inspiring work-space, set clear goals, and network like a pro. Be aware that you're not just imagining your success—you're living it. And who knows, maybe one day, you'll be the one inspiring other writers to achieve their dreams, all while sipping coffee and surrounded by a furry entourage.

2

Visualization for Achieving Goals

THE SUCCESSFUL AUTHOR uses visualization as an effective way to help manifest their goals and dreams. By focusing on the end result and immersing yourself in the emotions associated with achieving your goals, you can align your thoughts and actions with your deepest desires. Let's explore how you can use visualization to reach your career goals.

To harness the full potential of visualization, start by setting aside a few minutes each day to vividly imagine your ideal writing life. Visualize yourself signing book deals, receiving glowing reviews, and building a loyal fanbase that loves your work. Imagine earning a steady income from your writing and seeing your books in the hands of enthusiastic readers.

Engage all your senses—see the cover of your bestseller, hear the applause of your readers, and feel the joy of achieving your dreams. The more detailed and emotionally charged your visualization, the stronger its impact.

Visualization not only boosts your motivation but also helps you identify the steps needed to be successful and prosperous. By regularly visualizing your success, you create a mental blueprint that guides your actions and attracts opportunities aligned with your author career goals and I believe you'll one day become the successful author of your dreams.

Tips for Effective Visualization

- Focus on the End Result: When you visualize, concentrate on the final outcome, not the how. Imagine the book launch, the reader reviews, or the bestseller list—whatever your goal is as if it has already happened.

- Create a Quiet Space: Find a calm, quiet place where you can visualize without distractions. This helps you immerse yourself fully in the experience. (Or play soothing music in the background.)

- Be Specific and Detailed: Visualize every detail of your success. See the cover of your book, imagine the emails from enthusiastic readers, and visualize the sales numbers.

- Intensely Feel the Emotions: The more you can feel the joy, excitement, and satisfaction, the more powerful your visualization will be.

- Visualize Daily: Make visualization a daily practice. Dedicate a few minutes each day to your visualization practice. The more consistently you do it, the more you align your mind with your goals.

Visualizing 1,000 Pre-Orders

I had a goal to get one thousand pre-orders for my upcoming book. Now, this was no small feat, and the idea of reaching that number felt both exhilarating and daunting.

Every morning, I'd sit on my bed, close my eyes, and start visualizing. I didn't focus on the marketing strategies or the "how" of reaching one thousand pre-orders. Instead, I visualized the moment I'd see that magical number on my sales dashboard and the satisfaction of knowing my hard work was paying off. These visualizations were incredibly vivid, and the emotions felt real and immediate. I imagined the excitement of sharing the news with my family and friends, and even the celebratory dance in my office.

I let myself really feel those emotions—the joy, the thrill, the sense of accomplishment. It was like my future self was giving me a sneak peek into that glorious moment. And let me tell you, it felt fantastic. I even visualized the quirky little celebration I'd have with my cats, who, of course, were more interested in treats than my cool dance moves.

Day by day, I immersed myself in this emotional high, and then something amazing happened. My actions naturally aligned with my vision. I started coming up with creative marketing ideas, connecting more with my readers, and finding new ways to promote my book. It was as if my mind had become a magnet, attracting the right opportunities and people to help me reach my goal.

Then, one unforgettable morning, I logged into my sales dashboard and there it was: one thousand pre-orders. The excitement was overwhelming! The emotions I had been visualizing every day were now my truth. I did my little victory dance (yes, the cats were there too), and I felt a rush of gratitude and happiness.

Through this experience, I learned the true power of visualization. By focusing on the end result and feeling the emotions associated with my goals, I was able to manifest them into reality. Visualization isn't just daydreaming; it's an incredible practice that aligns your mind with your desires and motivates you to take inspired action.

And so, take a few minutes each day to visualize your author goals. See them as already achieved and feel the emotions that come with that success. Trust in the process, and watch as your dreams unfold before your eyes. And a little victory dance never hurts—just make sure your cat or dog approves!

3

Meditation/Prayer for Achieving Success

TAKE a moment to visualize what success looks like for you. Close your eyes and see yourself at your peak as a successful author—what does that feel like? Are you holding a freshly printed book with your name embossed on the cover? Are you receiving glowing reviews from readers who were moved by your story? Maybe you're giving a talk at a writer's conference, sharing your insights with eager newcomers.

The law of attraction teaches us that what we focus on expands. By clearly defining your version of success, you set a powerful intention that guides your actions and decisions. You align your energy with your goals, making them more attainable.

In the pursuit of a successful author career, one of the most valuable tools at your disposal is the practice of meditation and/or the power of prayer.

The Successful Author uses these practices to tap into the concept of the law of attraction, which states that by focusing on positive thoughts and desires, you can bring about corresponding positive results in your life.

This chapter will guide you through the process of using meditation and/or prayer to align your mindset with your writing goals, cultivating a positive, productive, and successful author career.

Tips for Effective Meditation on Writing Goals

- Find a Quiet Space: Select a place where you can sit comfortably without interruptions. This could be a comfy corner in your home, a serene spot in nature, or even a dedicated meditation room.

- Set a Clear Intention: Before you begin, take a moment to clearly define what you want to achieve. Whether it's finishing a novel, finding inspiration for a new story, or achieving bestseller status, having a clear goal in mind is crucial.

- Visualize Your Desired Outcomes: Close your eyes and imagine your goals as if they have already been achieved. See yourself holding your published book, receiving positive reviews, or signing books for enthusiastic readers. Engage all your senses in this visualization to make it as vivid as possible.

- Stay Consistent: Meditation and/or prayer are most effective when practiced regularly. Set aside a specific time each day to meditate and visualize your goals, even if it's just for a few minutes.

My Meditation and Writing

While writing this, I am reminded of the transformative power that meditation and prayer have had on my own writing career. I was stuck, utterly bogged down, like a fly in a honey jar. The ideas were buzzing around in my head, but the motivation and clarity? Nowhere to be found. That's when I decided to give meditation a whirl.

Every morning, I would retreat to a quiet spot in my garden, close my eyes, and start visualizing my goals. I imagined the thrill of completing my novel, the joy of seeing my name on the bestseller list, and the satisfaction of touching readers' lives with my stories. These weren't just idle daydreams; they were my mental bootcamp, aligning my thoughts and actions with my deepest desires.

One experience stands out clearly, mostly because it was a combination of outright panic and startling enlightenment. I was working on a novel that felt like trying to untangle Christmas lights—frustrating and seemingly impossible. The plot was a mess, and I was teetering on the edge of giving up and running away to join the circus. But then, during one especially soothing meditation session, I had a breakthrough.

As I visualized the completed manuscript, it was like the plot elves came to my rescue. New ideas flowed into my mind, and suddenly, solutions to plot holes and character issues appeared as if by magic. The fog lifted, and clarity breezed in, as if to say, "Hey, remember me?"

From that day forward, my writing time was more productive and inspired. I finished that story, which, much to my surprise and delight, went on to become one of my most successful fiction novels. Meditation didn't just boost my creativity; it also instilled a sense of calm and confidence that infused every aspect of my writing process. It was like having a personal cheerleader in my head, minus the pom-poms.

If you ever find yourself stuck, keep in mind that sometimes all it takes is a bit of quiet time, a cozy spot, and a dash of imagination to turn things around. And maybe the plot elves will visit you too.

Incorporating meditation and/or prayer into your routine can have a profound impact on your writing career. By lining up your thoughts with your goals and maintaining a positive, focused mindset, you can unlock your full creative potential and achieve the success you desire.

Meditation wasn't just a ritual; it aligned my inner self with my outer goals, bridging the gap between desire and reality. Every session cleared my mind, boosted my focus, and enhanced my creative output.

"Believe in your goals," I often tell other writers. "Visualize them with clarity to reinforce your intentions."

The Universe listens. And when you align your energy with your aspirations, magic happens.

4

Setting and Achieving Career Ambitions

THE SUCCESSFUL AUTHOR sets career goals because they know they are crucial for success. It's not just about dreaming big but also about planning strategically and staying focused. Establishing clear, practicable goals provides direction and motivation. Start by defining your long-term vision—whether it's becoming a bestselling author, securing a literary agent, making more money from your publications, or self-publishing a series.

Break this vision down into smaller, actionable steps, such as completing a manuscript, attending writing workshops, or building a professional online presence. Regularly review and adjust these goals to stay aligned with your evolving career goals. By maintaining a balance between ambition and practicality, and remaining adaptable to industry changes, you'll be better equipped to become a successful author.

Writing Down Your Goals

- Start by grabbing a journal and jotting down your top ten career goals. These can range from finishing your first novel to landing a publishing deal, or even becoming a keynote speaker at writing conferences. Writing down your goals makes them tangible and keeps them at the forefront of your mind.

Once you have your list, prioritize which goal should be your main focus. Ask yourself, "Which goal, if achieved, would make the biggest impact on my career right now?" This becomes your primary goal, the one that deserves most of your time and energy.

Setting Achievable Goals

- Achieving a big goal can often feel overwhelming. That's where objectives come in. Break down your main goal into smaller, manageable steps. For example, if your goal is to finish a novel, your intentions could include outlining the plot, writing each chapter, and completing revisions.

- Assign deadlines to each goal to keep yourself on track. Deadlines create a sense of urgency and help you measure your progress. Plus, there's nothing more satisfying than crossing off a completed goal in your journal!

Breaking Goals into Easy Steps

For each task, identify obtainable steps you can take. These should be specific objectives you can accomplish in a short amount of time. Instead of "write chapter one," try "write 1,000 words on chapter one." This makes your intentions less discouraging and easier to tackle.

The Power of Clear Objectives

Let me take you back to a pivotal moment in my writing career. I had just finished writing my first draft of a fiction novel. But the manuscript was a hot mess—characters went missing plots dangled without resolution, and let's not even talk about the pacing. I was about ready to toss it in the trash and call it a day.

Then, I grabbed my journal. I sat down and wrote out my goal: "Transform this disaster into a polished manuscript ready for self-publishing." It felt like climbing Everest in flip-flops, but I knew I needed a clear intention.

I broke this mammoth goal into bite-sized pieces. First, I tackled character development. I listed each character, their backstories, and motivations. Each day, I focused on one character, making them as real and three-dimensional as my favorite coffee shop barista who knows my order by heart.

Next, I addressed the plot holes. I created a detailed outline, plotting each chapter and ensuring every storyline tied up neatly, and that the pacing was improved—frustrating but incredibly satisfying when the pieces finally fit.

Throughout this time, I set deadlines for each goal. Revising character arcs by the end of the month, finishing the outline in two weeks, and so on. These deadlines kept me accountable and enthused.

I had a goal to finish the revision by my birthday. It was an ambitious target, but I was determined. And the day I hit that goal—there was an awkward celebratory dance, and copious amounts of chocolate cake. Not only had I transformed my manuscript, but I had also proved to myself that with clear objectives and focused effort, I could achieve anything I set my mind to.

The experience taught me valuable lessons. Firstly, breaking down big goals into smaller actions makes them less intimidating. Secondly, setting deadlines creates a sense of urgency that drives productivity. Lastly, celebrating achievements keeps the experience enjoyable and rewarding.

With this in mind, grab that journal, start writing down your goals, and map out your pathway to success. Every big achievement starts with a single step—and perhaps a piece of chocolate cake as a reward!

5

Attract Money and Level Up
Your Career

Your prosperous writing career awaits, and the Universe is ready to help you achieve it.

Attracting and manifesting money through the law of attraction involves aligning your thoughts, emotions, and actions with financial abundance. The Successful Author understands that to draw money into their life, they must first believe they are deserving of wealth and capable of achieving it. This starts with visualizing financial success, such as imagining royalty checks arriving, seeing their bank account grow, and feeling the security and freedom that comes with financial stability.

Affirmations like "I am financially prosperous" and "Money flows to me effortlessly" help reprogram the subconscious mind to embrace wealth. Also, expressing gratitude for both the money you have and the financial success you anticipate strengthens this belief and raises your vibrational frequency. By focusing on abundance and taking inspired actions, such as marketing your books effectively and exploring new income streams, you will create a powerful magnetic force that attracts wealth and abundance into your life.

I suggest believing in your worth and capabilities, so you can open yourself up to opportunities for growth and financial success. Visualizing success, practicing positive affirmations, and setting clear, achievable goals are powerful tools to help shift from a mindset of scarcity to one of wealth.

And I recommend keeping a gratitude journal that can help shift your focus from what you lack to the abundance already present in your life. I advise regularly writing down the things that you are grateful for, so you can train your mind to notice and appreciate the positive aspects of your life. This shift in focus raises your vibrational frequency, aligning you with the energy of prosperity. The law of attraction teaches that what you focus on becomes attracted to you, so by concentrating on gratitude, you allow more positive experiences and abundance into your life. Over time, this habit of gratitude helps to rewire your brain, making it easier to maintain a positive mindset and overcome certain limiting beliefs that may arise.

Tips to Attract and Manifest Money

- Set Clear Financial Goals: Define exactly how much money you want to earn and by when. Clear, specific goals help you focus your energy and actions toward achieving financial success.

- Visualize Abundance: Spend a few minutes each day visualizing your financial success. Visualize royalty deposits in the amount you want to manifest (for me it's $5,000.00 a month right now), your bank account filling with payments, and enjoying the benefits of financial freedom. Feel the emotions associated with this abundance.

- Use Positive Affirmations: Repeat affirmations such as "I am financially prosperous," "Money flows to me easily and effortlessly," and "I attract wealth and abundance." This helps reprogram your subconscious mind to concentrate on success.

- Express Gratitude: Keep a gratitude journal and regularly write down things you are grateful for, including your current financial situation and the wealth you are attracting. Gratitude raises your vibrational frequency and attracts more prosperity.

- Stay Open to Opportunities: Be on the lookout for new ways to generate income. This could be through book sales, speaking engagements, writing workshops, or freelance writing gigs. Stay open to diverse opportunities that can boost your earnings.

- Invest in Yourself: Allocate resources to improve your skills and knowledge. Taking courses, attending workshops, and investing in marketing can enhance your career and lead to greater financial returns.

- Create Multiple Income Streams: Diversify your income by exploring various avenues such as eBooks, audiobooks, merchandise, or book translations. Multiple streams of income can provide financial stability and abundance.

- Network and Collaborate: Build relationships with other authors, publishers, and industry professionals. Networking can lead to new partnerships and increased visibility for your work.

- Maintain a Positive Money Mindset: Cultivate a healthy attitude towards money. Avoid negative thoughts like "I can't afford this" or "Money is hard to come by." Instead, think positively about your financial future and the value of your work.

- Take Inspired Action: Actively work towards your financial goals by marketing your books, engaging with readers, and consistently producing quality content. Inspired actions taken with a positive mindset are powerful ways to manifest money.

Applying this advice, you can align your thoughts, emotions, and actions with financial abundance, attracting and manifesting the money you desire as an author.

Tips for Overcoming Limiting Beliefs

- Identify Your Limiting Beliefs: Reflect on thoughts that might be holding you back, such as "I can't make a living from writing" or "I'm not good enough." Write them down and challenge their validity.

- Replace with Positive Affirmations: Counteract limiting beliefs with positive affirmations like "I am a successful author" and "My writing attracts abundance."

- Visualize Success: Spend time each day visualizing your goals and the successful career you desire. See yourself thriving as an author.

- Seek Support: Surround yourself with supportive people who believe in your potential and encourage your career.

A Tale of Money Manifesting

Like many authors, I had my fair share of doubts about becoming a full-time author. I remember thinking, "Who am I kidding? Making a living from writing? That's just a farfetched dream."

I'll never forget the time I decided to put the law of attraction to work for my finances. It all started one morning when I was sipping my coffee, surrounded by my cats, who were clearly plotting world domination—or at least the overthrow of my keyboard. Sitting there, I realized that while my book sales were steady, I wanted to take my financial success to the next level. So, I decided to fully incorporate the principles of attracting and manifesting money into my life.

First, I set a clear financial goal: I wanted to triple my monthly income within six months. I wrote it down and visualized it every day. I visualized my bank account balance never going below $5,000.00 dollars (my goal at the time), the relief of paying off bills without a second thought, and treating myself to that ridiculously over-priced but oh-so-tempting writing desk I'd been eyeing.

I also started using positive affirmations. I plastered sticky notes around my office with phrases like "I am financially prosperous" and "Wherever my creativity flows, money goes" and "I'm so grateful to be a bestselling author of romance and mysteries." In the beginning, it felt like I was preparing for an amateur theater audition, but after a while, I started to believe my own words. My cats, of course, were unimpressed and continued their reign of terror over my workspace.

Gratitude became my secret weapon. Every evening, I jotted down things I was grateful for, from the loyal readers who shared my books online with other readers to the simple pleasure of a perfectly baked brownie. I even expressed gratitude for future successes, like my upcoming book hitting a new sales milestone.

Then, something magical happened. I noticed a significant increase in my newsletter subscribers and started attracting new readers to my romance pen name. It was as if the Universe had opened the floodgates of abundance, and I was finally reaching a broader audience with my work.

Through this experience, I learned that attracting and manifesting money isn't just about thinking positively—it's about believing in your worth, expressing gratitude, and taking inspired actions. By aligning my mindset and efforts with my financial goals, I not only improved my author fiction business, but also found greater happiness and fulfillment in my work.

Attracting and manifesting money as a writer is about more than just dreaming—it's about believing in your worth, expressing gratitude for what you have, and taking inspired action toward your goals. I suggest incorporating these principles into your life, so you can align your mindset with financial abundance and open the door to limitless opportunities.

So, to all the authors out there: set those big, bold financial goals, visualize your success, and watch as the Universe conspires to make your dreams come true.

6

Allowing Process with Manifestation

THE SUCCESSFUL AUTHOR understands that accelerating the manifestation process involves more than just setting intentions; it requires specific methods to align with your desires and attract them into your life faster. The law of attraction teaches that by focusing on positive thoughts, feelings, and actions, you can speed up the allowing process and live your author dream life that much faster. Implementing these manifestation techniques will help you stay aligned with your goals and make your dreams a reality.

- One powerful method is visualization

The Successful Author regularly visualizes their success in vivid detail, imagining book signings with long lines of fans, receiving glowing reviews, and seeing their books on bestseller lists. By immersing yourself in these positive images, you create a strong emotional connection to your goals, which helps to manifest them into your reality. Another effective technique is using affirmations.

Repeating positive statements about your success reinforces your belief in your abilities and helps to reprogram your subconscious mind to focus on achieving your dreams.

- Use the Pillow Method

The Pillow Method is a simple yet effective technique to help you manifest your desires. Write down your goals or affirmations on a piece of paper and place it under your pillow at night. This practice helps to imprint these desires into your subconscious mind, allowing them to take root while you sleep. By doing this, you create a continuous loop of positive reinforcement, keeping your goals at the forefront of your thoughts even during rest. The consistent focus on your aspirations helps align your energy with your desires, making it easier to manifest them into reality.

- Make Positive Statements

Speaking and thinking in positive terms is crucial for maintaining a high vibration and attracting success. Replace any negative self-talk with positive statements that affirm your success and abilities. For instance, instead of saying, "I can't do this," switch to, "I am capable and confident." These positive affirmations help to reprogram your subconscious mind, shifting your belief system towards one of empowerment and possibility. By consistently making positive statements, you reinforce a mindset of success and abundance, which in turn attracts more positive outcomes into your life.

- Be Clear About What You Want

Clarity is key when it comes to manifesting your desires. The Successful Author knows the importance of being specific about their goals and aspirations. The more precise you are in defining what you want, the easier it is for the Universe to understand and bring it to you. Instead of vaguely wishing for success, detail exactly what that success looks like for you by writing it down. Whether it's hitting a certain number of book sales, landing a particular publishing deal, or receiving specific accolades, clearly defining your goals helps to focus your energy and intentions, making manifestation more effective.

- Focus on the End Result, Not the 'How'

One of the core principles of the law of attraction is to concentrate on the outcome you desire rather than how you will achieve it. Trust that the Universe will guide you to your goal. When you concentrate too much on the 'how,' you can become bogged down by details and doubt, which may hinder your progress. Instead, visualize and feel the emotions of having already achieved your desired outcome. This practice keeps your vibration high and aligned with your goals. By maintaining this focus on the end result, you allow the Universe to work its magic and bring the necessary resources and opportunities your way.

- Feel the Emotions of Receiving

Feeling the emotions of receiving your desires is a powerful way to manifest your goals. Immerse yourself in the feelings of joy, gratitude, and satisfaction as if you have already achieved what you want. This emotional alignment is key to manifestation because it signals to the Universe that you are ready and open to receiving your desires. When you vividly imagine the fulfillment of your goals and truly feel the associated positive emotions, you create a strong vibrational match to your desires, accelerating their manifestation into your reality.

- Stay Vibrationally Aligned

Staying vibrationally aligned means maintaining a high vibration by focusing on positive thoughts, feelings, and actions that resonate with your desires. The Successful Author understands that their energy must match the energy of what they wish to attract. By consciously choosing positivity and engaging in activities that uplift you, you keep your vibration high and in tune with your goals. This alignment not only makes you feel better but also magnetizes you to the opportunities and resources needed to achieve your dreams. Regular practices such as meditation, gratitude journaling, and surrounding yourself with positive influences are essential for maintaining this high vibrational state.

- Remain in the State of Having

Remaining in the state of having involves consistently living in the mental state of already possessing what you desire. This mindset shift helps to draw your desires into your reality more quickly. When you think, act, and feel as if your goals are already accomplished, you align your energy with the end result, making it easier for the Universe to bring your desires to fruition. This approach removes any sense of lack or neediness, replacing it with a sense of abundance and fulfillment. By embodying the state of having, you become a powerful attractor for your goals, allowing them to manifest more smoothly and swiftly into your life.

- Feel Gratitude Daily

Gratitude is another essential component in accelerating the allowing process. The Successful Author makes it a habit to express gratitude not only for current achievements but also for future successes as if they have already happened. This practice shifts your focus from lack to abundance, raising your vibrational frequency and making it easier to attract your desires.

Recap on Ways to Accelerate the Allowing Process

- Believe in Yourself: Have unwavering faith in your abilities and your potential for success. Self-belief is a powerful catalyst for manifesting your desires.

- Use the Pillow Method: Write down your goals or affirmations on a piece of paper and place it under your pillow at night. This helps to imprint these desires into your subconscious mind.

- Make Positive Statements: Speak and think in positive terms. Replace any negative self-talk with positive statements that affirm your success and abilities.

- Be Clear About What You Want: Clearly define your goals and desires. The more specific you are, the easier it is to attract what you want.

- Focus on the End Result, Not the 'How': Concentrate on the outcome you desire rather than how you will achieve it. Trust that the Universe will guide you to your goal.

- Act as If You Already Have Success: Behave and make decisions as if you are already the successful author you aspire to be. This mindset attracts the reality you envision.

- Feel the Emotions of Receiving: Immerse yourself in the feelings of joy, gratitude, and satisfaction as if you have already achieved your goals. This emotional alignment is key to manifestation.

- Stay Vibrationally Aligned: Maintain a high vibration by focusing on positive thoughts, feelings, and actions that align with your desires.

- Practice Scripting: Write detailed scripts of your life as if your dreams have already come true. Describe your successes and daily experiences vividly.

- Remain in the State of Having: Consistently live in the mental state of already having what you want. This helps to draw your desires into your reality more quickly.

I recommend combining all of these methods, so you can effectively align with your goals and manifest your dream author life more quickly.

My Allowing Process

I remember the time I decided to accelerate my manifestation process to take my writing career to the next level. Not too long ago, I was sitting at my desk, surrounded by half-empty coffee cups, crumpled papers, and my cats strategically placed on my desk as if guarding some ancient literary secret. My sales were decent, but I knew I was capable of so much more. So, I thought, "Why not go all-in with this law of attraction stuff?"

First, I embraced visualization with the gusto of a kid at Disneyland. I imagined book signings with lines so long, they'd put a Black Friday sale to shame. I visualized myself on bestseller lists, receiving fan mail, and watching my bank account overflow as royalties poured in.

I'd spend a few minutes each morning with my eyes closed, sipping my coffee, and seeing these vivid scenes play out in my mind. Honestly, if my neighbors peeked in, they might have thought I was practicing some weird new form of coffee yoga.

Then, I dove into affirmations. I scribbled positive statements on sticky notes and plastered them all over my office. "I am a bestselling author." "My words inspire millions." "I always find my missing socks." (Okay, maybe not that last one, but you get the idea.)

After a while, these affirmations started to sink in. I found myself believing in my success more and more.

But the real catalyst was gratitude. I jotted down things I was grateful for in my notebook. Some days it was easy:

"Grateful for a productive writing session," "Grateful for supportive readers," "Grateful my cat didn't knock over my coffee today." Other days, I had to dig deep, like being grateful for spellcheck after a particularly rough spelling of "pseudonym." I even started expressing gratitude for future successes, writing things like, "Grateful for my upcoming book hitting the Amazon bestseller list."

Then, one day, after weeks of diligently following these practices, I checked my KDP dashboard sales report and saw that my sales had tripled that month. I nearly spilled my coffee on my keyboard in excitement. My visualizations were coming true! My dream of being a full-time author was becoming a reality, and being able to support my family through my writing was the icing on the cupcake.

Implementing these manifestation techniques didn't just improve my writing career; it transformed my mindset and daily life. I felt more positive, more creative, and genuinely excited about the future. So, to all my fellow writers out there: embrace your inner successful author, visualize like your life depends on it, affirm with confidence, and always, always be grateful (even if it's just for your pet or children or significant other not disrupting your writing time). Your dream author life is closer than you think!

7

Surrounding Yourself with Likeminded People

ONE OF THE most significant influences on your author career is the company you keep. The Successful Author surrounds themselves with like-minded, supportive individuals can propel you towards your dreams, while negative, unsupportive people can hold you back. It's crucial to be discerning about who you share your aspirations with, ensuring you're surrounded by those who lift you up, not bring you down.

The Successful Author builds a supportive network of likeminded writers, mentors, and enthusiastic readers that can significantly enhance their progress. Engage with writing communities, both online and offline, to find individuals who understand your challenges and commend your successes. The Successful Author attends writing workshops, joins critique groups, and participates in literary events to expand their circle. These connections can offer valuable feedback, encouragement, and even collaborative opportunities that can enhance your work.

Additionally, having a mentor that provides guidance and insights can be invaluable. On the other hand, you must be cautious of those who consistently criticize or doubt your potential, as negativity can erode your confidence and hinder your creativity. Prioritize relationships that inspire and motivate you, creating a positive and empowering environment that fuels your way to success.

Choosing Your Circle Wisely

The importance of befriending big-minded people cannot be overstated. These are the dreamers, the doers, and the believers. They see potential where others see problems; however, small-minded people are often stuck in their own limiting beliefs and can project their fears and doubts onto you.

Also, be careful about sharing your dreams with everyone. Not everybody in your life will understand or support your vision. Negative and unsupportive individuals can plant seeds of doubt, making you second-guess yourself. Instead, seek out those who encourage and inspire you.

Finding Supportive Communities

In today's digital age, finding a supportive community is easier than ever. Look for Facebook groups, online forums, or local writing clubs where positivity and encouragement abound.

Here are a few tips:

- Join Writing Groups: Look for groups specifically for writers. These can be found on Facebook, LinkedIn, or specialized writing platforms. Ensure the group's culture is positive and supportive.

- Attend Writing Workshops and Conferences: These events are goldmines for meeting like-minded individuals who share your passion and drive.

- Network Locally: Join local writing clubs or attend meet-ups. Face-to-face interactions can lead to deep, supportive connections.

Finding Your Tribe of Positivity

Early in her career, an author named Cathy was surrounded by a mix of supporters and naysayers. At the time, she didn't realize how much the negative voices were affecting her. She'd share her ambitious plans to draft a bestselling novel, only to be met with skeptical looks and comments like, "That's a tough industry," or "Maybe you should have a backup plan."

These comments started to chip away at her confidence. She began doubting her abilities and her dreams. But one day, after yet another discouraging conversation, she had an epiphany: she was allowing small-minded people to dictate the size of her dreams. Subsequently, she made a bold decision—she unfriended the naysayers, both in real life and on social media. It was like spring cleaning for her soul.

With the negative voices gone, Cathy sought out a tribe of positivity. She joined several writing groups on Facebook, attended local writing meet-ups, and even participated in a couple of writing retreats. She found herself surrounded by people who not only believed in their own dreams but also cheered loudly for hers.

Then at a writing workshop, she met a group of incredibly supportive authors who encouraged her to pitch her book idea to a publisher. Their belief in her gave her the courage to go for it. To her astonishment, the pitch was successful, and she landed her first publishing deal. That moment was a turning point in her career, all because she was surrounded by big-minded, positive individuals who believed in her potential.

The experience taught Cathy a valuable lesson: the people you surround yourself with can either be your anchors or your wings. Choose wisely. Seek out those who lift you higher, who applaud your victories, and who remind you of your potential when you forget it yourself.

Now take a look at your current circle. Are they lifting you up or holding you back? If it's the latter, it might be time for a little spring cleaning of your own. Remember, your dreams are precious. Protect them by surrounding yourself with people who support and encourage your business. Trust me, your future self will thank you.

8

Getting Organized and Decluttering Your Life

A CLUTTERED SPACE can lead to a cluttered mind. For the Successful Author, maintaining an organized workspace, schedule, and time management routine is crucial for productivity and creativity.

Begin by decluttering your physical workspace: remove unnecessary items, organize your writing paraphernalia. Invest in storage solutions that keep essential materials within reach but out of the way, such as shelves, drawers, and filing systems. A tidy space can reduce distractions and help you focus better on your writing.

Next, develop a schedule that aligns with your peak productivity times, setting aside dedicated writing sessions free from interruptions. Use calendars, planners, and apps to track deadlines, plan projects, and allocate time effectively.

Lastly, the Successful Author personalizes their workspace with inspiring elements, such as artwork, quotes, or plants, to create an atmosphere that stimulates creativity and helps keep you encouraged. By maintaining an organized and inspiring work area, you can enhance both your productivity and creativity, allowing you to write more efficiently and with greater focus.

An organized office sets the stage for success. It reduces distractions, develops a calm mindset, and allows for a more efficient workflow. Let's dive into practical tips for creating a tidy, efficient, and inspiring writing environment.

Here are some specific techniques to help you keep your workspace tidy and effective:

- Use Labeled Folders: Keep all your documents in labeled folders. This includes research notes, drafts, contracts, and other important papers. Digital folders on your computer should be equally organized.

- Set Daily or Weekly Writing Goals: Having clear goals helps maintain focus and direction. Write down your daily or weekly writing targets and keep them visible. This could be a word count goal, a chapter to complete, or time spent writing.

- Establish a Consistent Routine: Create a writing schedule and stick to it. Consistency helps build momentum and integrates writing into your daily life as a non-negotiable part of your routine.

- Keep a Clean Desk: At the end of each day, take a few minutes to clear your desk. A clean workspace can boost your mood and productivity the next time you sit down to write.

- Use Organizational Tactics: Invest in tools like planners, notebooks, calendars, or to-do lists. These can help keep track of deadlines, writing sessions, and other important tasks.

Transforming My Writing Space

My desk used to look like a tornado had hit it. Papers were everywhere, notebooks in a wobbly tower, guides on the craft stacked precariously near my keyboard like a Jenga tower, and random post-it notes stuck to every surface. I convinced myself that this chaotic workspace was the hallmark of a creative mind. But in reality, it was just an excuse for being disorganized.

One unusually hectic day, I couldn't find a crucial research note amidst the chaos. After spending an hour searching, I realized I had to make a change. My productivity and sanity depended on it.

For this reason, I was on a mission to declutter and organize my writing space. I started by investing in a set of sleek, labeled folders. One for research, one for drafts, one for contracts, and so on. Each paper found its rightful place, and suddenly, my desk seemed to breathe a sigh of relief.

Next, I tackled my digital space. I created folders on my computer with the same categories and organized all my files accordingly. No more searching through a mess of untitled documents. Everything was just a click away.

I also set up a routine. Every morning, after my cup of coffee, I'd sit down and write for two hours. No distractions, no excuses. It became a sacred time, and the consistency worked wonders for my productivity.

But the real difference-maker was setting daily goals. Each evening, I'd jot down what I aimed to achieve the next day. Sometimes it was a word count goal, other times it was to finish a chapter or edit a section. Having these goals gave my writing sessions direction and purpose.

The transformation was incredible. Not only did my productivity improve, but my creativity also thrived. With a clear, organized space, my mind was free to wander and create without the constant nagging feeling of disorder.

One specifically awesome moment came when I completed a novel ahead of schedule. The process was smoother, less stressful, and far more enjoyable. I even had time to cuddle with my cats amid a clean desk and a clear mind.

So, if your writing space resembles a disaster zone, take a step back and assess what needs to change. Invest in some folders, clear your desk, set those goals, and stick to a routine.

Trust me, the benefits are well worth the effort. Your future self—and your writing—will thank you. And who knows, you might even find that long-lost research note or discover that a tidy space makes room for big ideas.

9

Journaling for Your Author Career

ONE OF THE most transformative way to become a successful author is having a notebook or journal. By journaling daily about your author career goals and what you feel grateful for, you create a powerful practice that keeps you empowered and aligned with your aspirations. Let's dive into the benefits of journaling and how to make it a cornerstone of your writing career.

Writing down your goals and things you are grateful for creates a wonderful space for goal setting and manifestation, in line with the teachings of the law of attraction. By focusing on positive thoughts and expressing gratitude, you attract more of what you desire into your life. This practice helps the Successful Author stay aligned with their highest aspirations and intentions.

By writing down your goals and breaking them into feasible steps, you harness the power of the law of attraction to manifest your desires. This process creates a clear roadmap that guides your daily actions and long-term plans. Make it a habit to jot down not only your goals but also the successes you envision. This practice aligns your energy with your dreams and attracts success.

In addition to setting goals, incorporating a gratitude list into your journaling practice can amplify its benefits. Each day, take a moment to jot down at least three things you're grateful for, related to your writing journey and beyond. This simple yet powerful habit shifts your focus to the positive aspects of your life, developing a sense of appreciation and contentment.

Gratitude journaling helps the Successful Author stay grounded and recognize the progress and support they have, even in demanding times. By acknowledging the victories and blessings, you form a positive mindset that fuels creativity and resilience, making it easier to stay empowered and inspired.

The Importance of Daily Journaling

Journaling is more than just writing down your thoughts; it's a strategic practice for setting and achieving your goals while cultivating a positive mindset through gratitude. Here are some reasons why you should start journaling today:

- Clarity and Focus: Writing down your goals helps clarify your vision and keep you focused on what truly matters.

- Motivation: Seeing your goals in black and white can be incredibly motivating, especially on days when you feel stuck.

- Reflection: Journaling allows you to reflect on your progress, understand what's working, and identify areas that need adjustment.

- Accountability: A journal acts as a personal accountability partner, reminding you of your commitments.

- Gratitude: Incorporating gratitude into your journaling helps you appreciate your achievements and the support you have, fostering a positive and resilient mindset.

Setting Specific Goals

I suggest being specific and intentional with your goals. Start by writing out at least ten specific goals you want to achieve in the next six months.

These goals can include:

- Finishing a book

- Increasing book sales

- Building up a newsletter

- Expanding your reader base

- Attending writing workshops

- Improving social media engagement

- Securing a literary agent

- Launching a new book series

- Participating in author events

- Enhancing your writing skills

- Setting up your website or blog

- Rebranding your backlist with fresh covers, blurbs, keywords, etc.

Using the Journal as Inspiration

Take this step seriously. Your journal is not just a record of your dreams but a practical means for achieving them. Use it to set goals, track progress, and reflect on your career. Write daily, even if it's just a few sentences, to keep the momentum going.

And one way to bring more good things into your life is through gratitude. Start by writing out things that you are grateful for each day. Here are some ideas to get you started:

- The supportive community of readers and writers around you.

- Positive feedback and reviews from readers.

- The joy of seeing your book in print.

- The inspiration that flows into your writing.

- The ability to work from home and set your own schedule.

- The opportunity to share your stories with the world.

- The tools and resources that help you write and publish.

- The growth and progress you see in your writing.

- The encouragement from family and friends.

- The victories and achievements in your author career.

- The financial rewards and security from your writing career.

- A supportive community of fellow writers and readers.

- The software that make writing and publishing easier.

- Critique partners who help you improve your work.

- Access to research materials and resources that enhance your work.

- The companionship of your beloved pets while you write.

- Writing software that facilitate the creative process.

My Experience with Journaling

Journaling my goals and gratitude lists transformed my writing career and mindset. Like many people, I had watched the movie "The Secret" and it changed my life. The film introduces the concept of manifesting your desires through positive thinking and gratitude, which really resonated with me. Inspired, I decided to put these principles into action. I started by buying a beautiful leather-bound notebook to use as my goal/gratitude journal.

After watching the movie (about ten times!), I decided to get serious about journaling. I had read about the benefits of writing down your goals and expressing gratitude, so I thought, why not give it a shot?

Every morning, I start my day by jotting down at least ten things I am grateful for in my life. These ranged from the support of my amazing critique partners to the joy of having a reliable computer. I also wrote out specific goals I wanted to achieve in the next six months. They ranged from finishing my latest novel to increasing my newsletter subscribers and expanding my reader base.

I also began writing out my goals, both immediate and future. I listed things like ""Increase my book sales by 50%," and "Land a spot on a bestseller list."

But I didn't just stop there. I took a leap of faith and started thanking the Universe in advance for goals that hadn't happened yet. Every morning, I'd write, "I'm so grateful for the increase in book sales" and "Thank you, Universe, for the incredible success of my latest release."

At first, it felt a bit odd, almost like writing fanfiction about my own life. But I stuck with it, and something amazing started to happen. My mindset shifted. Instead of focusing on what I didn't have, I began to see the abundance in my life. I found myself more empowered and positive, even on days when my writing felt like slogging through molasses. Sometimes I even added things to my journal like: *Note to self: bribing yourself with a cookie for every 1,000 words written is surprisingly effective.*

One morning, as I was scribbling away in my journal, one of my cats knocked over my coffee (thanks, Kuromi). As I cleaned up the mess, I laughed. Even in moments of chaos, I felt a profound sense of gratitude. And wouldn't you know it, within a few months, my book sales started to climb. I received more positive reviews and even landed an unexpected feature in a popular book blog.

Through this practice, I learned that expressing gratitude for both current blessings and future successes can be incredibly empowering. It not only kept me optimistic and empowered but also made me more resilient in the face of setbacks. By believing in my goals and thanking the Universe in advance, I opened myself up to greater possibilities and abundance.

I encourage you to grab a journal and start writing down your goals and gratitude lists. Don't be afraid to thank the Universe for the successes you know are on their way. Trust me, it's a game-changer. And if a cat knocks over your coffee in the process, I believe a little humor and a lot of gratitude goes a long way.

10

Creating Your Dream Vision Board

THE SUCCESSFUL AUTHOR has a vision board. They understand that it's great way to help you visualize and achieve career goals. By assembling images and words that represent your dreams, you create a tangible reminder of what you are working towards.

To create an effective vision board, start by gathering images, quotes, and other materials that resonate with your author career goals. These might include pictures of your dream book cover, snippets of inspiring reviews, or photos of financial success symbols like stacks of money or royalty checks. Arrange these elements on a board or in a digital format where you can see them daily. As you place each item, take a moment to visualize yourself achieving that particular goal, feeling the emotions associated with your success.

Keep your vision board in a place where you'll encounter it frequently, like your writing space, to constantly reinforce your dreams. Regularly update your board to reflect your evolving goals and achievements, keeping your motivation fresh and your focus sharp. By consistently engaging with your vision board, the Successful Author will align their subconscious mind with their desires, making it an effective catalyst for turning any author dreams into actuality.

The Power of a Vision Board

A vision board helps you clarify your goals and keep them at the forefront of your mind. It serves as a visual representation of your dreams and a constant source of inspiration. Whether you print out pictures from the internet, cut out images from magazines, or create a private Pinterest board, the process of creating a vision board is both fun and empowering.

Here's how you can use a vision board to manifest your ideal author success life.

TIPS FOR CREATING Your Author Vision Board

- Gather Supplies: Get a large board, scissors, glue, and a collection of magazines or printouts. If you prefer digital, create a private Pinterest board.

- Visualize Your Goals: Think about what leveling up your author career looks like. Is it hitting bestseller lists, earning a steady income from book sales, seeing your sales numbers increase, or receiving positive reviews and fan mail? Visualize these goals clearly and in detail.

- Select Images and Words: Choose images and words that resonate with your goals. Like inspiring quotes, stacks of money, positive reviews, your book cover with a bestseller tag, or even symbols of financial success like luxury items, vacations, or anything else that represents your vision of a successful author career and increasing book sales.

- Place Your Vision Board Prominently: Keep your vision board where you can see it daily. It will serve as a constant reminder of your goals and keep you empowered.

How a Vision Board Can Help You Achieve Your Goals

I'd like to share an experience from a self-published author, Jeff, about his vision boards. Jeff has always been a fan of visual aids, so creating a vision board felt like a natural extension of his goal-setting process. In fact, he's created not just one, but several different vision boards over the course of his career.

The first vision board Jeff made was during a time when his writing career was in a decline. He filled it with images of book covers, author events, and inspiring quotes. One prominent image was of a book signing event with a long line of readers waiting for autographs— a scene he desperately wanted to experience.

Every day, Jeff spent a few moments looking at his vision board, allowing himself to feel the excitement and joy of achieving those goals. He even added a bit of humor to it, with a picture of a ridiculously fancy pen that he vowed he'd use for his book signings. It became a ritual that kept his spirits high and his focus sharp.

Fast forward seven months, and things started to shift. Jeff got invited to his first book signing event, and while the line wasn't as long as in the picture, it was a start. The feeling of accomplishment was immense. That ridiculously fancy pen? He bought it as a celebration gift to himself.

His second vision board focused on increasing book sales and expanding his readership. Jeff included images of bestseller lists, positive reviews, and graphs showing upward trends. Again, the power of his vision board came through. His sales started to climb, and his reader base grew significantly. The vision board kept him focused on marketing approaches and connecting with his audience.

Through these vision boards, Jeff learned valuable lessons. First, the act of creating a vision board helps you clarify what you truly want. Second, seeing your goals daily keeps you inspired and aligned with your dreams. Lastly, the practice of visualization, combined with consistent action, can lead to significant breakthroughs.

Start by gathering your supplies and creating your vision board. Let your imagination run wild, and don't be afraid to dream big. Trust me, it's a fun and amazing way to keep your goals front and center, and who knows, you might just find yourself honoring those achievements with a ridiculously fancy pen, too!

11

The Magnificent Power of Gratitude

GRATITUDE IS a transformative practice that can shift your mindset and attract more positivity into your life and career. The Successful Author concentrates on what they're thankful for to align with the abundance of the Universe. One effective way to cultivate gratitude is by creating a grateful list.

Begin by setting aside a few minutes each day to jot down things you are grateful for, no matter how big or small. This could include personal achievements, supportive friends and family, or even simple pleasures like a good cup of coffee. By regularly updating your grateful list, you train your mind to focus on the positive aspects of your life, which can boost your mood and motivation.

Reflecting on your list can also provide a sense of perspective during challenging times, reminding you of the progress you've made and the support you have. As your list grows, you'll find that this practice not only enhances your overall outlook but also attracts more opportunities and positivity into your author career. Gratitude truly acts as a magnet for abundance, implementing a mindset that is open to success and fulfillment.

To amplify the benefits of your grateful list, take a moment to truly, deeply feel the emotions of gratitude as you write each entry. Imagine the warmth and joy that each blessing brings to your life. I recommend immersing yourself in these positive feelings, you raise your vibrational frequency, which according to the law of attraction, helps you align with the abundance of the Universe. This emotional alignment not only boosts your mood but also acts as a powerful signal to the Universe that you are ready to receive more of the good things you are grateful for. As you consistently practice this, you'll notice that your heightened vibrations attract more success, opportunities, and fulfillment into your author career.

Here's how to do it and why it's so powerful.

Why Practice Gratitude?

Gratitude helps you appreciate what you have, reducing stress and increasing happiness. It can improve your overall outlook on life, making you more resilient and positive. For authors, it's especially beneficial as it nurtures a positive mindset essential for creativity and productivity.

Creating Your Grateful List

- Get a Journal or Notebook: Dedicate a special journal or

notebook to your gratitude practice. This makes the activity feel more intentional and meaningful.

- Daily Gratitude Practice: Find time each day to reflect on what you're grateful for. Write down at least 10 things you're thankful for each day for thirty days. This could be anything from a positive review, a kind comment about your writing, your computer, your cover designer, or even your favorite coffee shop.

- Be Specific and Varied: Don't just repeat the same things every day. Look for new things to be grateful for. This keeps your practice fresh and engaging.

- Feel the Emotions: After writing your gratitude list, read it out loud. Feel the emotions of gratitude and appreciation as you recite each item. This amplifies the positive impact of the practice.

Examples of What to Include

- A glowing review from a reader

- Positive feedback from a writing group

- The support of family and friends

- Your reliable computer or writing software

- A beautiful book cover designed just for you

- The joy of writing itself

- Access to research materials and books

- The satisfaction of hitting a writing breakthrough

- The peace and quiet of your writing nook

- The excitement of new ideas and inspiration

- Gratitude for an increase in book sales

- Thankful for a successful promo or ad

My Daily Gratitude

As someone who occasionally plots bookish domination (usually over a cupcake), I've found that practicing gratitude has had a profound impact on my writing career.

A while back, I was feeling a bit down about my progress. My latest book wasn't selling as well as I'd hoped, and I was starting to doubt myself. That's when I decided to focus on my gratitude journal. Each day, I'd sit down with my journal and write out whatever I was grateful for.

At first, it felt a bit forced. I mean, how many times can you be grateful for your cat not walking across your keyboard during a crucial scene? But soon, I found myself noticing more things to appreciate.

One day, I wrote about a lovely review a reader left, praising my book for its engaging characters and plot twists. Another day, I expressed gratitude for my plot-hole-finding editor, who turned my book into something enjoyable and readable. Another time, I thanked God and the Universe for a big increase in book sales that helped remind me not to give up.

I also started jotted down anything and everything I was thankful for, whether it was the amusing banter between a few of my readers and me online, the supportive words of a fellow author, or the purring of my cats as they lounged nearby. This practice helped me shift my focus from what was lacking to what was already abundant in my life. I began to feel more content and fulfilled, which naturally boosted my creativity and enthusiasm for writing.

As the days went by, I noticed a shift in my mindset. Instead of worrying on what wasn't working, I started appreciating all of the things that I often took for granted, like my computer and the manuscript formatting software that made my life so much easier.

One morning, as I read my gratitude list out loud, I felt a wave of positive emotions wash over me. I realized how lucky I was to be able to do what I love every day. This shift in perspective didn't just make me feel better; it also boosted my creativity and productivity. I started writing more, and to my surprise, my sales began to pick up. It was as if the Universe was responding to my gratitude.

Through this practice, I learned that gratitude is not just a feel-good exercise; it's the easiest and most powerful way to attract positivity and success. By focusing on what I was thankful for, I opened myself up to more of the same. My writing improved, my business grew, and I felt more connected to my readers and the writing community.

What are you waiting for? Get a journal, and start writing down what you're grateful for, and watch how it transforms your life and career. I believe that the Universe is always paying attention. Make sure it hears you appreciating all the good things you have, and it will surely send more into your life. And don't forget to savor a cupcake or two along the way—you deserve it!

12

Writing Schedule for Improved Productivity

THE SUCCESSFUL AUTHOR knows if you don't make writing a priority, you'll never finish a book. It's as simple as that. I've heard stories of authors taking ten years to write their first book. *Ten years!* That's a lot of wasted time and untapped potential. I suggest one way to avoid this fate is to establish a writing schedule and stick to it.

To be a successful author, you need to write often. Aim for at least five days a week. Whether you're an early bird or a night owl, find the time that works best for you and make writing a non-negotiable part of your routine. If you want to publish often, you need to write consistently.

Here are some tips to help you fit writing time into your busy schedule and make the most of it.

Fitting Writing Time into Your Schedule

- Set a Specific Time Each Day: Choose a time of day when you're most alert and creative. Whether it's early in the morning before the world wakes up or late at night when the house is quiet, carve out a dedicated time for writing.

- Create a Writing Ritual: Establish a routine that signals your brain it's time to write. This could be as simple as brewing a cup of tea, lighting a candle, or playing a particular playlist. Rituals help you transition into writing mode more smoothly.

- Use a Planner: Schedule your writing sessions in a planner or calendar, just like you would for any important appointment. Treat these sessions as sacred and non-negotiable.

- Establish Certain Goals: Define what you want to achieve in each writing session. Whether it's a word count goal, completing a chapter, or editing a specific section, having clear objectives keeps you focused and productive.

- Break It Down: If the idea of writing for several hours straight feels overwhelming, break it down into smaller, manageable chunks. Try writing in 25-minute intervals with 5-minute breaks in between (also known as the Pomodoro Technique).

- Eliminate Disruptions: Create a distraction-free environment. Turn off notifications, close unnecessary tabs, and let people know you're unavailable during your writing time.

- Be Flexible, But Consistent: Life happens, and sometimes you need to adjust your schedule. That's okay. What's important is that you remain consistent over time.

If you miss a session, don't stress—just get back to it the next day.

Prioritizing Writing and Achieving Goals

There was a time when I used to publish a book every year or two. While I was proud of each book, I knew I had more stories to tell and that I could be more productive. Because of this, I decided to make writing a top priority.

I committed to writing at least four to five hours a day, five days a week. This wasn't always easy, especially with the usual life distractions and occasional bouts of writer's block. But I treated my writing sessions like important meetings with myself—meetings I couldn't afford to miss.

My schedule was simple but effective. After breakfast, my mediation, visualization, and journaling, I'd make a strong cup of coffee, and sit at my desk by 8 a.m.

At first, it was a bit of a struggle. There were days when the words didn't flow and moments when I questioned my sanity for wanting to become a full-time author. I mean, who needs sleep anyway, right? But over time, I found my groove. Consistency paid off. I started writing faster and with more confidence.

Within a year, I managed to publish four books. Yes, you read that right—four books in one year. I couldn't believe it either! Especially, compared to my previous pace, this was nothing short of a miracle, for me anyway. Not only did my productivity increase, but the quality of my writing improved as well. I was more in tune with my creative process and more disciplined in my approach.

This experience taught me several valuable lessons. First, making writing a priority transforms it from a hobby into a career. Second, consistency is vital. Regular writing sessions, even when short, build momentum. Lastly, having a schedule doesn't stifle creativity—it enhances it. Knowing that I had dedicated time each day to write freed me from the guilt of not writing and allowed my creativity to flow more easily.

If you're serious about your writing career, create a schedule and stick to it. Find the time and make it a priority. Writing isn't just about putting words on a page —it's about honoring your passion and commitment to your craft. Plus, you might end up surprising yourself with how much you can accomplish.

13

The Power of Outsourcing

As an author, your primary focus should be on writing. However, the business side of being a successful author often demands a significant amount of time and energy. From marketing to social media management, these jobs can easily eat into your precious writing time. This is where outsourcing comes in. By hiring others to handle some of these responsibilities, you can free up time to devote to your writing. However, it's crucial to be careful and strategic when hiring help.

Why Outsource?

Outsourcing allows you to delegate projects that are important but not directly related to writing. This could include book marketing, social media management, graphic design, editing, or administrative duties. By outsourcing, the Successful Author can focus on what they do best—writing.

Tips for Hiring Help

- Get References: Before hiring anyone, make sure to check their references. Speak to others who have used their services to ensure they are reliable and competent.

- Clear, Upfront Agreements: Be clear about what you need done and when. Outline specific assignments, deadlines, and expectations in writing. This prevents misunderstandings and ensures everyone is on the same page.

- Regular Check-Ins: Have your hires report back to you upon the completion of each project or task. Regular updates help you stay informed and ensure the work is progressing as planned.

- Quality Over Cost: Don't just go for the cheapest option. Sometimes, paying a bit more for a professional service can save you time and headaches in the long run.

Lessons from a Hiring Misstep

About seven years ago, I decided to hire someone to handle my social media marketing because, frankly, I needed to free up time for writing and stop spending hours scrolling through cat memes. I found someone who seemed perfect— professional website, impressive pitch—and paid them upfront for a month's worth of work. What could possibly go wrong?

Well, to say I was disappointed would be an understatement of epic proportions. Weeks went by with little to no updates. The few posts they did manage to put up were so lackluster, even my cats were unimpressed. By the end of the month, I realized I had basically flushed that money down the drain. The grand total of my social media engagement? A few likes from my kids and one from an enthusiastic spam bot.

This experience taught me a few valuable lessons. First, always get references and do your homework before hiring anyone. Just because someone has a fantabulous website doesn't mean they're competent; it just means they're good at making websites. Second, be clear about your expectations and have everything in writing. Ambiguity can lead to misunderstandings and unmet expectations, like when I said "engaging content" and they heard "post whatever you feel like." Finally, regular check-ins are crucial. Had I insisted on weekly updates, I might have caught the problem sooner and been able to course-correct before my social media presence flatlined.

Despite this setback, I didn't give up on outsourcing. I became more diligent in my hiring process and eventually found a fantastic virtual assistant who, unlike her predecessor, actually understood the concept of 'work.' She took care of my social media and other mundane endeavors, letting me focus on my job—writing. By delegating tasks, I was able to publish more books that year.

I suggest being careful when hiring help. Outsourcing can be helpful and beneficial for your productivity, but only if done right. Take the time to find the right people, set clear expectations, and maintain regular communication. Your writing career—and your sanity—will thank you.

In conclusion, don't be afraid to seek help. Remind yourself that you're not just an author; you're also running a business. Freeing up time to focus on your craft is invaluable. With the right team supporting you, you'll have more time to enjoy the little things in life, like plotting your next bestseller or indulging in your favorite chocolate as a reward for all your hard work.

Positive Communication

IN TODAY'S DIGITAL AGE, the things we say and post online hold immense power. Joel Osteen said it best: "If you complain, you will remain; if you praise, you will be raised." This principle is at the heart of the law of attraction. When you spout negativity, you attract it into your life. Conversely, spreading positivity can lift you to new heights.

To harness this power, the Successful Author is mindful of their online presence and the energy they project. Share your successes, express gratitude, chat up your books and the work of others, and offer encouragement to writers in your community. Avoid engaging in negative rants or complaints. Instead, use your platforms to build a positive, supportive network that reflects the success you wish to achieve.

The author community can be incredibly supportive, but it can also be downright toxic. Unfortunately, some authors post public grievances, bully other authors, and belittle their peers. Don't be that author. Instead, focus on a positive and respectful online presence.

And please keep in mind that your readers are part of your online audience too. Posting negative content can affect them and their perception of you as an author. In my experience, readers want to connect with authors who inspire and uplift them, not those who spread negativity. Try to maintain a positive and professional online presence to strengthen your relationship with your readers and followers. This positive interaction can lead to stronger reader loyalty, more word-of-mouth recommendations, and ultimately, greater success in your writing career.

I recommend consistently sharing positivity because you not only rise your vibration but also attract like-minded individuals and opportunities that align with your intentions. This conscious practice can transform your digital interactions into a magnet for abundance and success.

The Impact of Words

If you say things out loud or post them online like, "My books are not selling," "I'll never be successful," "I never get any reviews," or "I'll never finish this book," you're essentially inviting those realities into your life. The Universe listens to your words and thoughts, so it's crucial to be mindful of what you communicate.

To flip the script, try this advice from author Terri Savelle Foy, every time you say something negative about your job, life, family, or anything else, I suggest adding:

"...and that's just the way I want it" to the end of the negative talk. For example, "I'll never be successful...and that's just the way I want it." If it's *not* the way you want your career or life to go, then don't speak it or post it into existence!

Tips for Positive Communication

- Reframe Negative Thoughts: Instead of saying, "My books aren't selling," try, "I'm working on new ways to reach my readers." This keeps your focus on positive action.

- Use Positive Affirmations: Replace negative statements with affirmations. For instance, "I am a successful author attracting readers every day."

- Avoid Complaints: Complaining publicly can attract more negativity. Instead, focus on what's working and express gratitude. (When you complain, you remain.)

- Engage Positively: Interact with others in a supportive and uplifting manner. Avoid any negative talk or posting. Be professional and handle most issues in private.

- Mind Your Online Presence: Be aware that what you post online can be seen by potential readers, publishers, industry professionals, and collaborators. Keep your online presence professional and positive.

Changing the Narrative

An author I know, Danica, used to vent her frustrations online. She'd post things like, "Why is no one buying my novels?" or "I'll never be a full-time author." It felt good to get it off her chest, but she didn't realize the impact it was having.

I shared with Danica the advice from Terri Savelle Foy to add on "...and that's just the way I want it" to any negative statement. Danica thought about it and realized how ridiculous her complaints sounded with that addition. Like stating, "I'll never finish this book...and that's just the way I want it." Of course, that's not what she wanted at all!

From that moment, Danica decided to change her narrative. Instead of complaining about slow book sales, she started posting about her family, pets, and any funny mishaps with characters trying to take over the plot. She replaced "I'll never finish this book" with "I'm making steady progress on my manuscript." She focused on the positive aspects and the steps she was taking to improve.

The shift was incredible. Not only did Danica feel more hopeful and positive, but she also noticed a change in her interactions. Readers started engaging more with her posts, offering encouragement and sharing their own experiences. Her writing productivity improved, and she even finished her manuscript ahead of schedule.

However, a few months later, Danica was feeling overwhelmed with a looming deadline and the anarchy of managing life with three dogs (who keep distracting her by begging treats, and barking at the poor mailperson). Instead of posting a complaint, she took a deep breath and wrote, "Making great progress on my book today, thanks to my furry muses and a strong cup of green tea!"

The response was overwhelmingly supportive, and she felt a renewed sense of determination.

This experience taught Danica that words have immense power. By changing how she communicated, both online and offline, she attracted more positivity and support into her life. It wasn't just about feeling good; it was about creating a reality that aligned with her goals and dreams.

With this in mind be conscious of your words. Speak and post with intention, focusing on positivity and progress. I believe the Universe is always listening. Make sure what it hears aligns with the life you want to create.

And if you ever feel the urge to complain, just remember to add, "…and that's just the way I want it." If it doesn't feel right, it's a sign to reframe your thoughts. Trust me, your future self will thank you.

Just remember, the energy you put out into the world is what you receive in return.

15

Visualizing Your Future Success

ONE OF THE primary ways you can level up is to visualize your future successful self. Imagine what your life will look like once you've achieved your dreams. How will you feel? How will you spend your days? What kind of books will you write? How will your readers respond to your work? What does your future life look like? What kind of financial abundance will you enjoy? How will you use your wealth to enhance your life and the lives of those around you? What kind of lifestyle will you lead with the success and abundance you attract?

Envision the book signings, the money you're attracting, the bestseller tag on your next publication, the glowing reviews, and the sense of accomplishment you'll feel. I recommend focusing on this image and feeling the emotions, so you can draw inspiration and motivation from your future self.

Take a few moments each day to vividly imagine yourself living your dream life as a successful author. See yourself holding your published books, signing copies for eager fans, and receiving accolades for your work. Feel the pride and joy of accomplishing your goals, and let these emotions fuel your daily efforts.

The clearer and more detailed your visualization, the more real it becomes in your mind. This practice not only keeps you determined but also aligns your energy with your goals, making it easier to attract the success you desire.

By regularly connecting with your future successful self, you reinforce your belief in your ability to achieve your dreams and attract the opportunities needed to make them a reality.

Let's dive a bit deeper into how you can harness this vision to propel yourself forward.

The Power of Future Visualization

Visualization is a significant principle of the law of attraction. When you clearly visualize your future successful self, you align your thoughts and actions with that reality.

Here's how to make this practice work for you:

- Create a Detailed Vision: Imagine your perfect day as a successful author. Where are you? What does your typical day look like? How do you feel? See every detail vividly.

- Feel the Emotions: It's not enough to see your future; you need to feel it. Experience the joy, satisfaction, and pride of living your dream.

- Listen to Your Future Self: What advice would your successful-self give you today? Perhaps it's to stay focused, stop wasting time, or to keep pushing forward despite challenges.

- Incorporate Daily Affirmations: Use affirmations that reflect your future success. Statements like "I am a best-selling author" or "I attract new readers around the world that love my books" can keep you motivated.

- Take Action: Visualization should inspire action. Use the image of your future self to guide your decisions and actions today.

Drawing Inspiration from My Future Self

I'll share a quick story about how visualizing my future successful self has made a significant impact on my career. I've always been drawn to the idea of using visualization to shape my reality.

A while back, my writing felt uninspired, and my author business seemed stagnant. One evening, while sipping my favorite coffee and pondering my next move, I stumbled upon a chapter in an inspirational book about visualizing your future self. The idea intrigued me, and I decided to give it a try.

I closed my eyes and imagined my life as a successful author. I pictured a cozy, sunlit writing nook filled with my favorite books and a purring cat on my lap. I saw myself typing away effortlessly, the words flowing like magic. I felt the thrill of receiving positive reader feedback and the pride of seeing my books on bestseller lists.

The emotions were so real that I could almost touch them.

But I didn't stop there. I asked my future self what advice she had for me. The response was clear: "Don't give up. Keep living the dream. Get more focused and stop wasting time. The sooner you get serious about your writing, the sooner you'll be living this reality."

Inspired by this vision, I decided to make some changes. I set specific goals and created a more disciplined writing schedule. I started each day with affirmations like "I am a successful author" and "I am so grateful to be a full-time author."

As I put this advice into practice, my writing became more focused and I made it a priority. I completed projects faster, published more often, and started making more money on book sales.

Once when I hit the Amazon top 100 bestseller list, I bought myself a new book (of course) and a special cupcake treat. The positive momentum continued, and I saw my book sales increase and my reader base expand over the next several months confirming I was heading toward my dreams.

Through this practice, I learned that visualizing your future successful self is more than just a motivational exercise—it's about aligning your present actions with your future goals. By focusing on the life you want to create, you can draw inspiration and guidance from that vision, helping you stay encouraged and on track.

Please take a moment to visualize your future successful self. Let that vision inspire and guide you. Listen to the advice your future self has to offer and put it into practice today. Understand that the way to success starts with a clear vision and the determination to become a profitable and productive author.

And if you ever need a little extra inspiration, there's always a new book waiting to be read and a future-self cheering you on.

16

Studying Successful Authors

ONE OF THE best ways to level up your author career is by studying what successful authors in your genre are doing. Pay attention to their strategies and tactics to understand what works. Are they posting frequently online? Publishing a book every month? Designing book covers that easily convey their genre? Hitting the right tropes? By observing and learning from these authors, you can adapt their effective practices to your own career.

Take this a step further by actively engaging with these successful authors and their communities. Most of them are very open about their successes and their failures, sharing what worked and didn't work for them. Follow the authors that you admire on social media, join their reader groups, and subscribe to their newsletters. (Just try not to come across as a stalker!) I recommend analyzing their interactions with fans and how they handle promotions and launches. Don't hesitate to reach out for advice; many authors are willing to share their insights and experiences. Additionally, invest time in reading their books to understand their writing style, plot structures, and character development.

By immersing yourself in their work and approaches to success, you'll gain valuable insights that you can tailor to fit your own career goals. This proactive approach will not only inspire you but also provide a roadmap to boost your own success in the competitive world of writing. Just remember that what works for one person might not work for you.

What to Study

- Online Presence: Notice how often they post and what kind of content they share. Are they engaging with their readers, sharing behind-the-scenes looks, or promoting their books effectively?

- Publication Frequency: Check how often they release new books. Some authors have a rapid-release strategy that keeps their audience engaged and eager for more.

- Book Covers: Look at their book covers. Are they genre-specific and appealing? A great cover can make a huge difference in attracting readers.

- Story Tropes: Successful authors often hit the right tropes that readers love. Study their books to understand what tropes are popular in your genre and how they are executed.

- Newsletter Strategy: A large, engaged subscriber list is a goldmine. See how they build and maintain their newsletter audience.

- Reviews: Read both positive and negative reviews. Positive reviews tell you what readers love, while negative reviews highlight what to avoid.

Learning from the Best

Let me share an account from an indie author, Bellamy, that emphasizes the importance of studying successful authors. Bellamy was always on the lookout for ways to improve his author business.

He started by identifying a few bestselling authors in his genre. He noticed one author, in particular, was publishing a book every month like clockwork. Intrigued, Bellamy dove deeper into her strategy. Her online presence was consistent and engaging, with a perfect mix of promotional content and personal anecdotes. Her book covers were always on point—each one a perfect representation of its genre.

Then, he moved on to her books themselves. This successful author hit all the right tropes, and her reviews were glowing. But it was the negative reviews that offered the most surprising insights. Readers pointed out issues that Bellamy could easily avoid in his own writing—like overused clichés or slow pacing.

Inspired by her approach, Bellamy decided to implement some changes. First, he revamped his online presence, making sure to post regularly and engage with his readers more actively. He shared snippets of his writing process, pictures of his dogs (always a hit), and even his favorite soup recipes.

Next, he tackled his publication schedule. While a book a month seemed nerve-wracking, so instead, he set a goal to release a new book every three months. This pace was more manageable for him but still frequent enough to keep his readers engaged.

Bellamy also took a hard look at his book covers. He realized they needed a bit of a makeover to better fit his genre. After revising his book covers, he saw an immediate improvement in sales and reader engagement.

Finally, he paid close attention to the tropes his target audience loved. He incorporated these elements into his writing while ensuring his stories remained unique and fresh. His books started to climb the charts, and his reader base grew significantly.

Through this process, Bellamy learned that studying successful authors isn't about copying them but about understanding what works and why. By adapting their mindset and success tactics to fit his own style and strengths, he was able to enhance his author business to new heights.

I recommend taking the time to study what the best in your genre are doing. Pay attention to their tactics, learn from their successes and mistakes, and apply these insights to your own career. I believe that success leaves clues. By following these clues, you can create your own way to success while sipping coffee and petting your furbaby.

17

Inspirational Reading Materials

READING inspirational stories and books on writing, marketing, editing, the law of attraction, money, and personal memoirs can be an empowered way to stay driven and improve your author career. These books can offer valuable insights, practical advice, and the motivational boost you need to keep pushing forward.

By immersing yourself in these inspirational stories and books, you not only gain knowledge but also connect with the experiences of others who have faced similar challenges. Highlighting significant takeaways and implementing the techniques you learn can provide possible ways to enhance your writing and marketing efforts. Furthermore, these readings can serve as a constant reminder that success is attainable with persistence and the right mindset.

Make it a habit to read inspirational stories regularly that resonate with your goals. This continuous learning process will keep you inspired, informed, and equipped to manifest your dreams and grow your author career effectively.

Let's explore why reading these types of books is essential and how it can enhance your career as an author.

Why Read Inspirational Books?

- Motivation: Reading about other authors' successes and challenges can inspire you to keep going, especially when you hit a rough patch.

- Knowledge: Books on writing, marketing, and editing provide practical tips and techniques that can improve your craft and business acumen.

- Mindset: Books on the law of attraction and money help you develop a positive mindset, essential for attracting success and abundance.

- Personal Growth: Inspirational memoirs offer valuable lessons and perspectives that can enrich your own life.

Recommended Reading

- Author Success Stories: Look for biographies and memoirs of successful authors. These stories can offer insight into the habits and mindsets that contributed to their success.

- Writing Craft Books: Books on writing techniques, story structure, and character development can help you hone your craft.

- Marketing and Business: Learn about book marketing, branding, and business procedures tailored for authors.

- Law of Attraction: Explore books that teach the principles of the law of attraction and how to apply them to your writing career.

- Inspirational Memoirs: Read personal memoirs that offer insights into overcoming obstacles and achieving dreams.

My Monthly Dose of Inspiration

As a self-proclaimed book hoarder who's been writing since the tender age of seven, I've always believed in the transformative powers of reading, and one practice that has profoundly impacted my business is enjoying a new inspirational book every month.

On one occasion, I hit a bit of a slump. My writing felt forced, and I was struggling to stay motivated. One day, while organizing my overflowing bookshelves, I stumbled upon a book about success and manifesting money. (Because who doesn't think a fat saving account isn't sexy? Trust me, it is.) Their memoir detailed their rise to wealth, the hurdles they faced, and the plans they used to overcome them to build up their business. Intrigued, I decided to make it my read for the month.

That book was a game-changer. I devoured it in a few days, feeling a renewed sense of purpose and inspiration. The author's story gave me the push I needed to keep going. Inspired by this experience, I made a pact with myself to read one inspirational book each month.

Since then, I've read a variety of books—some on writing techniques, others on marketing, and many on the law of attraction. I even dabbled in personal memoirs that weren't directly related to writing but offered valuable life lessons. Each book provided a new perspective, a fresh burst of motivation, and practical tips that I could apply to my own life and career.

For instance, one month I read a book on the law of attraction that emphasized the importance of visualizing your goals. I started incorporating visualization into my daily routine, imagining my books flying off the shelves and receiving glowing reviews. Another month, I read a guide on book marketing that introduced me to new methods for reaching readers.

Reading inspirational books became a nice ritual. Each story offered new ways to stay empowered. One book, in particular, emphasized the importance of surrounding yourself with positivity. Inspired, I joined a few online writing communities where members were supportive and encouraging. The positive energy was contagious and further boosted my determination to become a full-time author.

Through this practice over the last ten years, I've gained valuable clarity that has improved my life, my relationships, and my author business. I've learned new writing techniques, discovered effective marketing practices, and developed a more positive and happy mindset. Most importantly, I've been reminded time and again of the power of the Universe and the magic of believing in your dreams.

I encourage you to dive into the world of inspirational reading. Find books that speak to you and your life. Let their wisdom and stories fuel your ambitions to succeed.

Empower Yourself With Confidence

CONFIDENCE IS necessary in your writing career and author business. Empowering yourself with confidence can help you overcome obstacles, stay motivated, and reach your goals. The law of attraction teaches us that the energy we put out into the world is the energy we attract back. By choosing confidence, you set an optimistic tone for your business, drawing success and opportunities your way.

To cultivate this confidence, start by acknowledging your accomplishments, no matter how insignificant they may seem. Give yourself a high-five with each achievement, from finishing a chapter to receiving constructive feedback from a reader. Surround yourself with supportive people who believe in your potential and remind you of your strengths.

I recommend practicing positive affirmations daily, bolstering your belief in your abilities and your vision. Visualize your success, imagining yourself achieving your goals and thriving as an author. This practice not only boosts your self-esteem but also aligns your mindset with your dreams.

Confidence isn't about never feeling doubt; it's about choosing to move forward despite it. It's about believing in your abilities, trusting your decisions, and maintaining a determined mindset. As you consistently project confidence, you'll find that opportunities and success naturally gravitate towards you, reinforcing the powerful cycle of the law of attraction.

The Power of Confidence

Here's how you can empower yourself and boost your confidence in your writing career:

- Determine What Your Goals Are: Knowing what you want to achieve gives you a sense of direction and purpose. Set specific, feasible goals and create a plan to reach them.

-Positive Affirmations: Use positive affirmations to reinforce your confidence. Statements like "I am a successful author" or "I attract readers who love my work" can boost your self-belief.

- Honor Successes: Acknowledge and be proud of your achievements. This builds momentum and reinforces a positive mindset.

- Surround Yourself with Positivity: Engage with supportive communities, read inspirational books, and limit exposure to negative influences.

- Keep Learning and Growing: Continuously improve your skills through reading, courses, and practice. Knowledge boosts confidence and competence.

Choosing A Confidence Mindset

As someone who's been studying the law of attraction for over a decade (and still no way near being an expert... yet!), I've learned a thing or two about maintaining a confident mindset.

Many years ago, I was struggling with self-doubt. One morning, while sipping my coffee and contemplating life (as one does), I decided to take control of my mindset. I knew I had to choose confidence and empower myself to stay positive.

I started by setting clear goals. I wanted to finish my next book within three months and double my newsletter subscribers by the end of the year. These goals gave me a sense of direction and something tangible to work towards.

Next, I turned to positive affirmations. Every morning, after my workout, I'd stand in front of the mirror and say, "I am a successful author. My books inspire and captivate readers." And gradually, I started believing it. The affirmations helped me alter my mindset from doubt to confidence.

I also made it a point to feel proud of my hard work. When I finished a particularly challenging chapter, I treated myself to a cupcake (or two). When I received a positive review, I did a little happy dance with my cats.

These celebrations kept my spirits high and reminded me of my progress.

One day, as Halloween approached (my favorite holiday, of course), I decided to throw a spooky-themed online book launch. The response was overwhelming. Readers loved the idea, and my book sales spiked. This success reinforced the power of choosing confidence and staying positive.

Through this practice, I learned that confidence is a choice. By setting clear goals, using positive affirmations, rejoicing in every win, surrounding yourself with positivity, and continually learning, you can empower yourself to achieve your dreams.

Empower yourself with a positive mindset and believe in your abilities. Recognize the energy you put out, is the same energy you attract. Stay hopeful, keep pushing forward, and rejoice in your victories. And if all else fails, there's always a cupcake and a new book in your favorite genre waiting to lift your spirits.

19

Harnessing the Power of
Positive Affirmations

THE SUCCESSFUL AUTHOR knows that positive affirmations is a fun and inspiring way to help them stay empowered and purposeful in their author business. By writing affirmations down, posting them around your office or on your vision board, and saying them out loud, you can turn negative thoughts into positive ones and attract success into your life. Many successful people meditate, use affirmations, wake up early, and are lifelong learners.

Affirmations can transform your mindset and boost your author career. And affirmations are positive statements that help you overcome self-sabotaging and negative thoughts. When you repeat them often and believe in them, you can start to make positive changes.

The Successful Author realizes that affirmations work hand-in-hand with the law of attraction by aligning their thoughts and beliefs with their desired outcomes. When you consistently practice affirmations, you are essentially reprogramming your subconscious mind to focus on success and abundance. This change in mindset helps you to naturally attract opportunities that align with your goals.

I recommend visualizing and feeling the emotions tied to these positive affirmations, and you will raise your vibrational frequency, signaling to the Universe that you are open and ready to receive the success you desire. Over time, this practice not only changes your internal dialogue but also manifests substantial results in your author career, strengthening the power of positive thinking and belief.

Here's why affirmations are so powerful:

The Power of Affirmations

- Reprogram Your Mind: Repeating positive affirmations helps rewire your brain, replacing negative thought patterns with positive ones.

- Boost Confidence: Affirmations can boost your self-esteem and confidence, making you feel more capable and self-assured.

- Focus on Goals: They help you stay focused on your goals and maintain a positive outlook, even during challenging times.

- Attract Positivity: According to the law of attraction, the energy you put out into the Universe is what you attract. Positive affirmations help you emit positive energy.

How to Use Affirmations

- Write Them Down: Write your affirmations on sticky notes or index cards and place them where you'll see them often—on your desk, computer, mirror, or vision board.

- Say Them Out Loud: Speak your affirmations out loud with conviction. Hearing your own voice reinforces the message.

- Be Consistent: Practice your affirmations daily. Consistency is crucial to making them effective.

- Believe in Them: Truly believe in the affirmations you're saying. The more you believe, the more powerful they become.

The Impact of Affirmations

I firmly believe in the transformative power of affirmations, and I've found that affirmations have played a crucial role in my success.

Some time ago, I was in a bit of a rut. My writing wasn't flowing, and I was feeling overwhelmed by the demands of my author business. One morning, after a grueling workout session, I decided to change my approach. I had always believed in the power of positive thinking, but I hadn't fully incorporated using affirmations.

I started by writing down a few simple affirmations: "I am a successful author," "My creativity flows effortlessly," and "I am grateful for the financial abundance my writing brings me." I posted these affirmations around my office, on my vision board, and even on the fridge (a prime location, considering my frequent cupcake breaks).

Every morning, I'd say these affirmations out loud as part of my daily routine, adding more specific affirmations related to my goals, such as "I am always attracting new subscribers to my newsletter" and "My books are best-sellers."

At first, it felt a bit awkward, like talking to myself in the mirror. But gradually, I began to believe the words I was saying. My mindset started to shift, and I noticed a change in my energy and motivation.

The results were amazing. Not only did my productivity and creativity improve, but I also started seeing definite results in my author business. My newsletter subscribers increased, my book sales picked up, and I received more positive feedback from readers. It was as if the Universe was responding to the positive energy I was putting out.

One day, after reciting my affirmations, I had a break-through idea for a new book. The words flowed effort-lessly, and within months, I had completed a manuscript that I was incredibly proud of. When I published it, the response from readers was overwhelmingly positive, reaf-firming the power of affirmations and a positive mindset.

Through this experience, I learned that affirmations are more than just words—they are powerful ways to shape your reality. I suggest consistently practicing affirmations to transform your mindset, boost your confidence, and attract the success you desire.

Adopt the power of positive affirmations. Write them down, say them out loud, and believe in them. Let them guide you towards your goals and help you stay confident. Moreover, the Universe is always listening—make sure it hears you speaking your dreams into existence.

20

Mindful Posting and Commenting

THE IMPORTANCE of Professionalism Online

Social media can be a double-edged sword for authors. While it offers a platform to connect with readers and other writers, it can also become a venomous environment if you're not careful. A happy, successful, and positive person doesn't spread hate or negativity.

To maintain professionalism online, it's crucial to be mindful of what you post and how you interact with others. Always aim to contribute positively to discussions, offering support and encouragement rather than criticism or negativity. Avoid engaging in online arguments or sharing controversial opinions that could alienate your readers or peers. Instead, focus on sharing your achievements, promoting your work, and praising the successes of others.

By consistently projecting a positive and professional image, you not only attract more followers and potential readers but also build a reputation as a reliable and uplifting presence in the writing community. This approach not only aligns with the principles of the law of attraction but also promotes a supportive network that can enhance your career and personal growth.

I believe that the vibrational energy (good and bad) that you put out into the world is what you receive in return.

Here's how to stay professional and positive online.

The Power of Mindful Posting

- Avoid Spreading Negativity: Social media can be both uplifting and toxic. Avoid spreading hate or negativity. If you have a friend who has been wronged, offer comfort and support privately. Do not take up a pitchfork and lead the charge to discredit, belittle, attack, or harm another person. Bear in mind that there are usually two sides to every story, and karma is real. Be professional and kind.

- Handle Reviews Gracefully: If you get a bad review, don't whine or complain about it online. It's natural to feel hurt, but cry in private and seek support from friends or family. Do not out the reviewer or make a big deal out of it publicly. All authors receive some bad reviews; it's part of the journey. Remind yourself that it's just one person's opinion and doesn't define your worth as a writer.

- Focus on the Positive: Share uplifting and inspiring content. Be proud of your achievements, support fellow authors, and engage positively with your readers. By focusing on the positive, you create a welcoming and encouraging environment for yourself and others.

Navigating Social Media with Positivity

Let me share an example from an indie author, Heather, on her experience about the importance of mindful posting. Heather is always on the lookout for ways to improve her mindset and her author business. A while back, she received a harsh review on one of her books. It stung, and her initial reaction was to vent her frustration online. But then I offered her a piece of advice: "Your response to criticism shapes your future success." She decided to take a step back and handle the situation with grace.

Instead of posting a rant on social media, Heather called a close friend and poured her heart out. They shared a few laughs, ate some chocolate, and she felt much better. The next day, Heather took a deep breath and read through the review again, this time looking for constructive feedback. She found a few points that she could use to improve her writing, and she decided to focus on that instead of the negativity.

Around the same time, a friend of Heather's was involved in a social media conflict. Her friend had been wronged, and a part of Heather wanted to defend her publicly. But she knew that joining the online fray would only add fuel to the fire. Instead, Heather reached out to her friend privately, offering her support and listening to her side of the story. Her friend appreciated the approach, and they were able to discuss ways to handle the situation calmly and professionally.

Through these experiences, Heather learned the importance of staying professional and positive online. By choosing not to engage in negative behavior, she preserved her peace of mind and maintained her reputation as a positive and supportive member of the writing community.

I recommend focusing on positivity and professionalism to attract more of the same into your life. This mindset has helped many authors stay encouraged and inspired, even in the face of criticism.

Please be mindful of what you post and comment on online. Support your friends, but positively, encouragingly, and constructively. Handle negative reviews with professionalism, and focus on the positive aspects of your life. Your online presence and life are a reflection of who you are. Make sure it's one that attracts good karma, kindness, forgiveness, and gratitude.

21

Your Author Business Brand

ONCE YOU HIT 'PUBLISH,' you transition from writer to business owner. The Successful Author knows the importance of strong branding. Your brand is the face of your author business, and it encompasses everything from your professional bio to your website, social media presence, and even your book covers.

To build a cohesive and compelling brand, start by defining what makes you unique as an author—your voice, your themes, and the emotions you want your readers to experience. Use these elements to craft a professional bio that resonates with your audience and displays your personality and expertise. Ensure that your website is visually appealing and easy to navigate, with consistent branding elements like color schemes, fonts, and imagery that reflect your style. Your social media presence should align with this branding, providing a unified look and feel across all platforms.

Additionally, invest in high-quality book covers that not only attract readers but also communicate the essence of your stories. I recommend maintaining consistency and authenticity in all aspects of your branding, and you will create a strong, recognizable identity that sets you apart in the competitive publishing industry, attracting loyal readers and enhancing your overall success.

Here's how to build and maintain a cohesive and professional author brand.

The Importance of Author Branding

In the crowded world of publishing, having a unique, identifiable brand can set you apart from the competition. Branding is not just about aesthetics; it's about creating a memorable and trustworthy image that resonates with your audience. A well-crafted brand conveys professionalism, consistency, and a clear sense of who you are as an author.

Here's why branding is crucial for your success as an author:

- Professionalism: A cohesive brand presents you as a genuine, professional author. It shows that you take your career and your work seriously, which can attract more readers and media attention.

- Recognition: Consistent branding helps readers recognize your work at a glance. When your book covers, website, and social media all align, it's easier for readers to remember you, recognize your brand, and find your books.

- Trust: A professional brand builds confidence with your audience. When readers see a well-crafted brand, they are more likely to trust the quality of your work and invest in your books.

- Connection: Branding allows you to share your personality and values with your readers. It creates a connection that goes beyond your books, making readers feel more engaged and loyal.

- Marketing: A strong brand makes marketing easier and more effective. It provides a clear and consistent message that you can use across all your promotional efforts.

Essential Elements of Author Branding

- Professional Bio: Your bio is often the first introduction readers have to you. Make it engaging, informative, and reflective of your personality and writing style.

- Website or Blog: Your website is your online home. It should be professional, easy to navigate, and regularly updated. Include a blog to engage with readers and share insights into your writing process.

- Author/Business Logo: A unique logo helps readers identify your brand at a glance. Use this logo across all your marketing materials, including your website, social media, and book covers.

- Banners/Headers for Social Media: Consistent, professional banners and headers for your social media accounts create a cohesive look and reinforce your brand.

Ensure these graphics reflect your brand's style and genre.

- Professional Headshot or Logo: A high-quality headshot or logo adds a personal touch to your brand. Use it for your website, social media profiles, and promotional materials.

- Consistent Online Presence: Maintain a professional and consistent presence across all online platforms. Engage with your audience positively and regularly update your content.

Building My Author Brand

When I first started publishing, I thought my job was done once I hit 'publish.' I quickly realized there was much more to it. My online presence was scattered, my website was outdated, and I didn't have a cohesive brand. It was time for a change.

I started by revamping my professional bios. Instead of a dry, factual account, I injected some personality into each one of my pen names. I highlighted my love for books (being a book hoarder), my enthusiasm for the law of attraction, and my penchant for saving stray cats. This made my bios more relatable and engaging.

Next, I tackled my blog, which I use as my website. I uploaded a professional template I purchased on Esty to create a clean, modern site that reflected my style. I shared monthly updates on my writing, future publications, and whenever I updated a series with new book cover branding. This also helped me connect with readers on a deeper level.

Realizing the importance of a visual identity, I created new logos for all of my pen names as my headshot. Gone was the blurry selfie; in its place was a professional and fun logo of me that exuded confidence and approachability. I used this image on my website, social media, and even on promotional bookmarks. The logo image was striking yet distinctive, and I began using it across all my marketing materials. My social media profiles got a facelift with new banners and headers that matched my updated aesthetic. This consistency made my brand instantly recognizable.

One of the biggest changes was branding my book covers. I created covers that not only looked professional, but also conveyed the genre more easily. This consistency helped establish a strong brand identity.

The results were extraordinary. My online presence became more professional and cohesive, and my reader engagement improved. My books started to attract more attention, and I noticed an increase in sales. It was clear that a strong brand had made a significant impact on my author career.

Through this experience, I learned that branding is not just about aesthetics; it's about creating a memorable and trustworthy image that resonates with your audience. A well-crafted brand conveys professionalism, consistency, and a clear sense of who you are as an author.

For that reason, take the time to build and maintain your author brand. Invest in a professional bio, a well-designed website, a distinctive logo, and consistent branding across all platforms. Be aware that once you hit 'publish,' you are a business. And a successful author business thrives on strong, cohesive branding. Keep this in mind, update it when needed, and watch your author career prosper.

22

Perseverance in Your Career

PERSEVERANCE IS the key to success in any endeavor, especially in the world of writing. The Successful Author writes on a schedule and publishes books often. The more books you write, the more money you'll make. Groups on Facebook offer tons of free advice from trade published to bestselling indie authors, emphasizing the importance of consistency and purpose.

Perseverance also means understanding that setbacks are a natural part of the process. Rejection letters, slow sales, or writer's block can be discouraging, but they are not the end of the road. Each challenge is an opportunity to learn and grow. These moments are a part of your story, knowing that every successful author has faced similar obstacles. By persisting through the tough times, you build resilience and character, which ultimately strengthens your writing and your resolve.

The Importance of Perseverance

- Consistency Builds Momentum: Writing regularly and publishing frequently keeps your readers engaged and helps you build a loyal audience. It also improves your craft over time, as practice truly makes perfect.

- Increased Income: The more books you have available, the more potential income streams you create. Each new publication is an opportunity to attract new readers and generate sales.

- Professional Growth: Persevering through challenges and setbacks helps you grow as a writer. It teaches you to overcome any obstacles within the publishing industry.

- Learning from Others: Engaging with online communities can provide valuable insights and support. Learning from those who have endured similar situations before you can shorten your learning curve and inspire you to keep going.

Embracing Your Purpose

As a Developmental Editor, Ghostwriter, Book Cover Designer, and Plot Consultant/Creator, I wear many hats. My own fiction and non-fiction publications have graced the Amazon bestseller lists, but getting there wasn't always easy.

Inspired by the stories and advice from online forums and Facebook groups, I set a goal to write and publish more frequently to take my writing career to the next level.. I created a writing schedule and committed to sticking to it, no matter what.

At first, it was tough. Balancing my various roles while finding time to write felt like juggling flaming torches while riding a unicycle. But I persevered. I wrote every day, even if it was just a few hundred words. I designed my own book covers, ensuring they were professional and eye-catching.

One of the most challenging moments came when I was working on a complex mystery novel. The plot twists and murder suspects were giving me a headache, and I was tempted to put it aside. But I used the advice from the writing community: "Keep going. Write the next book." So, I pushed through the frustration, keeping my eye on the bigger picture.

When I finally hit the publish button, the sense of accomplishment was overwhelming. The book did well, climbing the Amazon bestseller lists and attracting positive reviews. Each book I published built upon the last, creating a steady stream of income and a growing reader base.

Through this experience, I learned that perseverance isn't just about writing more books; it's about maintaining a positive mindset and believing in your ability to succeed. It's about pushing through the tough times and applauding the victories.

Write on a schedule, publish often, and don't be afraid to learn from others. Engage with writer communities and take other successful authors' advice to heart. Remember, every word you write brings you one step closer to your goals. Keep pushing forward, and soon enough, you'll find yourself on the road to success.

And if you need a little extra motivation,: the more books you write, the more cupcakes you can justify eating as a reward.

23

Mental Blocks and Clarifying Your Goals

MENTAL BLOCKS CAN BE a major obstacle to becoming a successful author. They can stall your progress, sap your motivation, and make your dreams seem out of reach. However, a successful author works through any blocks that keep them from their dreams. Equally important is having crystal-clear goals and a detailed plan to achieve them. Clarity of purpose and the ability to overcome mental barriers are essential components of a thriving writing career.

Mental blocks often stem from self-doubt, fear of failure, or simply feeling overwhelmed by the sheer magnitude of your goals. It's crucial to identify these blocks and address them one at a time. Techniques such as meditation, journaling, or speaking with a mentor, a life (author) coach, or a friend can help you uncover the root causes of these barriers. Once identified, you can implement methods to overcome them, such as seeking support from other successful writers, or setting aside specific times for creative activities. Every successful author has faced mental blocks; the difference is in their determination to push through.

Being crystal clear on what you want to accomplish is the next vital step. This clarity helps you stay focused, make informed decisions, and measure your progress. Start by setting specific, measurable, achievable, relevant, and time-bound (SMART) goals. Know exactly what you want to achieve, whether it's completing a novel, increasing your readership, or hitting a sales target. Having a clear vision not only keeps you optimistic but also helps you stay focused.

Overcoming Mental Blocks and Clarifying Goals

- Identify Your Blocks: Take time to reflect on what's holding you back. Write down your fears and doubts, then work through each one with positive affirmations and constructive actions.

- Set SMART Goals: Make sure your goals are Specific, Measurable, Achievable, Relevant, and Time-bound. This clarity will keep you on track and optimistic.

- Break It Down: Divide larger goals into smaller, manageable tasks. This makes the process less overwhelming and allows you to observe all victories along the way.

- Seek Support: Join writing groups or find a mentor or life coach. Sharing your career with others can provide encouragement, accountability, and new perspectives.

Breaking Through Mental Blocks

Once upon a time, I found myself buried under a mountain of projects and plagued by imposter syndrome. My goals felt like distant dreams, almost as elusive as a cat that suddenly decides it doesn't want to be found (trust me, I know the type). It was clear I needed to clear my mental blocks to move forward.

I started by journaling every morning, writing down my thoughts and fears over a strong cup of coffee, which might be considered essential for both coherence and survival. This practice helped me identify the root of my mental blocks: a fear of failure and a lack of clear direction.

With this newfound awareness, I decided to break my goals into smaller, attainable projects. Instead of focusing on the challenge of finishing an entire book, I set a goal to write two thousand words a day. This simple change made my writing sessions more manageable and enjoyable, especially with my cats occasionally helping by pouncing on the keyboard.

I also created a vision board, which quickly became a decorative masterpiece adorned with images of successful book launches, positive reader reviews, and inspirational quotes. Every time I looked at it, I felt a surge of determination to keep pushing forward—much like how I feel when I see a mocha latte.

One time I set a SMART goal to design and publish a series of book covers within three months. Breaking this larger goal into weekly assignments, I tackled one cover at a time, which felt like unwrapping a new, delicious cupcake every week. The sense of accomplishment I felt with each completed cover was incredibly motivating. By the end of the three months, I had not only achieved my goal but also boosted my confidence and creativity to levels.

Through this process, I learned that clarity and perseverance (or my own stubbornness) are potent tools in an author's arsenal. By identifying and addressing my mental blocks and setting clear, practical goals, I was able to overcome obstacles and achieve success. This experience taught me that no matter how big your dreams are, with the right mindset and attitude, they are within reach. Plus, a healthy dose of coffee, a sprinkle of humor, and the occasional indulgence in cupcakes doesn't hurt either.

Please take the time to clear your mental blocks and be crystal clear about your goals. Every step you take brings you closer to your dreams. And if you ever need a little extra inspiration, just look at your vision board and remind yourself of the amazing future you're creating.

24

Establishing a 90-Day Writing Habit

CREATING a consistent writing habit is crucial for success as an author. A 90-day writing habit routine can transform your writing from an occasional hobby into a daily practice that's integral to your lifestyle. The purpose of this routine is to carve out a dedicated time for writing, ensuring that you make steady progress on your projects and develop the discipline needed to thrive in the competitive world of publishing.

A 90-day commitment is the perfect length of time to establish a new habit. It's long enough to make writing a natural part of your daily routine, but short enough to feel realistic for you.

By dedicating yourself to this practice, you'll find that writing becomes less of a chore and more of a fulfilling and essential part of your life. It's about showing up every day, rain or shine, inspired or not, to put words on the page. Over time, these consistent efforts will accumulate, leading to significant progress and a stronger writing discipline.

Tips for Creating and Sticking to a 90-Day Writing Habit:

- Set a Daily Writing Goal: Determine a realistic daily word count or time goal. Whether it's 1,000 words, or just 30 minutes of writing, commit to it every day.

- Choose a Specific Time: Find a time of day that works best for you and stick to it. Whether you're an early bird or a night owl or write during your lunch hour, consistency is important.

- Your Writing Space: Designate a specific place or two for writing. Make it comfortable and free from distractions.

- Use a Planner: Track your progress in a planner or journal. Seeing your streak grow can be incredibly motivating.

- Reward Yourself: Celebrate all accomplishments with rewards. Treat yourself to a favorite snack or a break to read a chapter of a book.

- Stay Accountable: Share your goals with a friend or join a writing group. Accountability can help keep you on track.

- Be Flexible: Life happens. If you miss a day, don't beat yourself up. Get back to your routine the next day.

Embracing a 90-Day Writing Habit

As someone who juggles multiple roles in the writing and publishing world, finding time to write can be a challenge. I realized that my sporadic writing schedule was holding me back. I needed a more disciplined approach, so I decided to commit to a 90-day writing routine.

I set a modest goal of writing five days a week. I figured this was manageable, even on my busiest days. I chose to write first thing in the morning, before the demands of the day could intrude. I had all my essentials: a comfortable chair, my favorite coffee mug, and a candle that smelled like creativity (or so I told myself).

The first week was tough. There were mornings when I would have preferred to stay in bed, but I dragged myself to my writing desk, coffee in hand. I soon found that the act of showing up was half the battle. Once I started typing, the words flowed more easily than I expected.

One memorable morning, about a month into my routine, I woke up feeling extremely uninspired. My cats were more enthusiastic about their breakfast than I was about writing. But I sat down and started anyway. To my surprise, what began as a reluctant session turned into one of my most productive writing days. I not only hit my word count but exceeded it, finishing a tricky chapter that had been bothering me for weeks.

By the end of the 90 days, writing had become a natural part of my daily routine. I had written more consistently than ever before and made significant progress on my projects. The discipline I developed during those 90 days carried over into other areas of my life, making me more organized and focused.

This experience taught me that establishing a writing habit is about more than just hitting word counts. It's about showing up for yourself and your dreams every day. It's about building momentum and creating a positive cycle of productivity and creativity.

I encourage you to try a 90-day writing habit. Set your goals, find your time, create your space, and commit to showing up every day. It might be challenging, but the rewards are well worth it. And every word you write brings you one step closer to your dreams.

25

The Financially Savvy Author

BEING a successful author isn't just about drafting compelling stories; it's also about being financially savvy and investing wisely in your career. The law of attraction teaches us that what we focus on expands, and this principle applies perfectly to managing your finances. By paying attention to your financial health and making strategic investments, you can create a sustainable and prosperous author career.

Financial smartness involves understanding your income and expenses, setting aside funds for future projects, marketing, and investing in resources that will enhance your writing and marketing efforts. A successful author knows the value of budgeting and planning. They keep track of their royalties, plan for taxes, and save for both expected and unexpected expenses.

Wise investments are crucial. This might mean spending money on a professional editor to polish your manuscript, hiring a designer for a professional book cover, or investing in advertising campaigns that increase your book's visibility. By allocating your resources wisely, you not only improve the quality of your work but also increase your chances of reaching a wider audience and boosting sales.

Tips for Financial Savviness

- Create a Budget: Outline your income and expenses. Track your royalties and plan for regular expenses like software subscriptions, marketing, and professional services.

- Save for Taxes: Set aside a portion of your income for taxes. This prevents financial stress when tax season arrives.

- Invest in Quality: Spend money on professional services like editing, cover design, and marketing. Quality investments can lead to higher sales and a better reputation.

- Build an Emergency Fund: Save money for unexpected expenses. This fund can provide a safety net during slow sales periods or personal emergencies.

- Continuous Learning: Invest in courses, guidebooks, and conferences that help you grow as an author and businessperson.

Financial Wisdom in Action

In previous years, I found myself overwhelmed by the financial side of my author business. My royalties were coming in, but so were the expenses, and I wasn't keeping track as diligently as I should have been. It all came to a head one tax season when I realized that I hadn't set aside nearly enough to cover my tax bill. I had to set up a payment plan, which was not an ideal situation.

Determined to never face that stress again, I decided to get financially savvy. I started by creating a detailed budget, tracking every dollar that came in and went out. I set up a separate savings account specifically for taxes and made it a habit to transfer a percentage of my income into that account every month.

One of the most enlightening investments I made was in a marketing course. The techniques I learned transformed how I promoted my books, leading to a significant increase in my readership and sales. The course wasn't cheap, but it paid off many times over.

Through these changes, I learned that being financially savvy isn't about being cheap; it's about making smart investments that will pay off in the long run. By managing my finances better and investing wisely, I improved my financial health and felt less stressed. Now, I can focus more on my writing, knowing that I have a solid financial plan in place.

I suggest you take the time to get financially savvy. Create a budget, save for taxes, invest in quality, and keep learning. Your future self—and your writing career—will thank you.

And with the right financial strategy, you can afford to spoil your pets and loved ones even more.

26

On the Right (Write!) Path

THE LAW of attraction teaches us that staying positive and focused on our goals attracts success and opportunities into our lives. The Successful Author understands that every word written, every rejection faced, and every challenge overcome is a step closer to achieving their dreams. They accept the business with all its ups and downs, knowing that diligence is necessary. They maintain a positive mindset, visualize their success, and continue to write even when the going gets tough. This resilience not only helps them improve their craft but also builds a strong foundation for a successful career.

The Successful Author also understands the importance of gratitude in the journey to success. By appreciating the lessons learned along the way, they raise their vibrational frequency and attract even more positive experiences. Gratitude helps them stay grounded and focused on their long-term vision. The Successful Author reinforces their commitment and motivation to keep pushing forward daily. This combination of resilience, positivity, and gratitude creates a powerful force that propels a writer toward their ultimate goals.

Tips for Staying on the Right Path

- Visualize Success: Regularly visualize yourself achieving your writing goals. Envision your books on bestseller lists, receiving glowing reviews, and touching the lives of readers.

- Stay Positive: Cultivate a positive mindset. Focus on what you can control and take pride in your hard work along the way.

- Set Realistic Goals: Break down your larger goals into manageable steps. This makes your career goals less overwhelming and keeps you enthusiastic.

- Seek Support: Surround yourself with a supportive community of writers and readers who encourage and inspire you.

- Keep Writing: No matter what happens, keep writing. Consistency and persistence are the keys to success.

Staying on the Right (Write!) Path

It's summer 2013, my favorite season, and I had just self-published my third YA urban fantasy novel, a book I was immensely proud of. Despite my excitement, the initial sales were, well, let's just say they were more crickets than roaring applause. But I remembered what the law of attraction teaches us—stay positive and focused, and the Universe will align with your desires.

Instead of wallowing in self-pity or giving in to the temptation of a chocolate binge (which, let's be honest, was very tempting), I decided to practice what I preach. I started each day with a visualization exercise, imagining my book climbing the bestseller lists, readers leaving mostly positive reviews, and the sales graph looking like a steep mountain peak. I even imagined my bank account swelling with each sale, which, I must admit, was a particularly delightful image.

But visualization was just the start. I also made a point to express gratitude daily. I thanked the Universe for the opportunity to share my stories, for the readers who had already discovered my books, and the professionals I worked with. I wrote these gratitude notes in my journal every morning, right before tackling my writing and other projects for the day.

This positive mindset was put to the test one particularly difficult week. I had a client for a cover design who was more indecisive than a cat choosing between two sunspots. Every change request felt like a tiny jab at my confidence. But instead of letting it get to me, I reminded myself to be grateful for the business. I thanked the Universe for this lesson in patience and creativity, and I kept visualizing my ultimate goal.

Then, something remarkable happened. Slowly but surely, sales started to pick up. My gratitude practice seemed to be paying off in more ways than one. Readers began to discover my book, leaving passionate reviews, and I even received a few emails from fans asking when my next book would be out. My client finally approved the book cover, raving about how perfect it was. That week, I saw a significant uptick in both book sales and new clients for my design services.

This experience reinforced the importance of staying positive, visualizing success, and practicing gratitude. It taught me that every word written, every problem faced, and every moment of appreciation brought me closer to my dreams.

The Universe has a way of rewarding those who believe in their dreams, and trust me, the rewards are sweeter than you can imagine. Keep going, stay positive, and never give up. The world needs your stories, and success is just around the corner.

Time Wasters to Boost Productivity

THE SUCCESSFUL AUTHOR knows that time is a precious commodity. With deadlines looming and stories to tell, it's crucial to identify and eliminate time wasters that hinder writing progress. If you're spending two hours every day watching TV or mindlessly scrolling through social media, that's valuable time that could be dedicated to writing. By being mindful of how you spend your time, you can create more opportunities to write and live your very best author life.

Time-wasting activities often creep into our schedules unnoticed. While a funny cat meme on TikTok might bring a moment of joy, it can easily turn into an hour-long distraction. The Successful Author is vigilant about recognizing these distractions and implementing ways to minimize them. This doesn't mean you have to give up all leisure activities, but rather find a balance that allows you to prioritize your writing. Setting specific times for relaxation and social media can help you stay focused and productive.

Tips for Identifying and Eliminating Time Wasters

- Track Your Time: Spend a week tracking how you spend your time. Identify activities that are taking up more time than necessary.

- Set Limits: Allocate specific times for activities like watching TV or using social media. Use timers to keep these activities in check.

- Create a Writing Schedule: Dedicate specific blocks of time each day to writing. Treat these times as non-negotiable appointments with yourself.

- Prioritize Tasks: Focus on high-priority projects and/or responsibilities first. If writing is your main goal, make it the first thing you do each day.

- Remove Distractions: Create a distraction-free writing environment. Turn off notifications, close unnecessary tabs, and let others know you're unavailable during your writing time.

- Use Productivity Tools: Apps like StayFocusd or Rescue-Time can help you limit time spent on distracting websites.

Overcoming Time Wasters

One day, an author friend of mine, Timothy, realized that his writing was suffering because he was spending too much time on social media. He would open Facebook to post an update, and before he knew it, an hour had passed, and all he had accomplished was laughing at funny cat videos. Then he'd play online games for another three hours.

Determined to reclaim his writing time, Timothy decided to track his daily activities. He discovered that he was spending nearly two hours a day on social media, three hours gaming, and another hour watching TV. It was a wake-up call. He knew he needed to make a change if he wanted to finish his manuscript on time.

Timothy started by setting limits on his social media usage and gaming hours. He allowed himself thirty minutes in the morning and thirty minutes in the evening to catch up on news and connect with friends. He used a timer to ensure he didn't go over his allotted time. For TV, he chose to watch only one episode of his favorite show each evening, rather than binge-watching for hours.

To further enhance his productivity, Timothy created a writing schedule. He blocked out two hours every morning exclusively for writing. He turned off his phone, closed all unnecessary tabs, and let his family know he was in "writing mode." At first, it was challenging to stick to this new routine. But as the days went by, he found himself looking forward to his dedicated writing time.

One particular morning, Timothy was tempted to check his email instead of diving into his manuscript. But he resisted the urge and focused on his writing. To his surprise, he finished a difficult chapter that day, one that had been giving him trouble for weeks.

By pinpointing and eliminating his time wasters, Timothy significantly increased his productivity. His writing sessions became more focused and fruitful, and he was able to complete his manuscript ahead of schedule. This experience taught him the value of being mindful of how he spends his time and the importance of prioritizing his writing.

I suggest taking a moment to evaluate your own daily routines. Identify the time wasters that are holding you back and minimize them. Plus, every minute you reclaim is a minute you can invest in your writing. Stay focused, stay productive, and watch your author career level up.

28

Author Self-Care

THE SUCCESSFUL AUTHOR knows that self-care and being kind to yourself is important. Writing is not just a mental exercise but also a physical and emotional one. The Successful Author understands that taking care of their mind, body, and spirit is crucial for sustaining creativity and productivity. This means prioritizing rest, nourishing your body with healthy foods, and engaging in activities that bring joy and relaxation. It's about recognizing that you're not a machine; you're a human with needs that deserve attention and care.

The law of attraction teaches that the energy you put into the Universe is the energy you receive back. By prioritizing self-care, the Successful Author ensures that they are in a positive, high-vibrational state, which in turn attracts more positive experiences and opportunities. When you take the time to rest, eat well, and engage in joyful activities, you are telling the Universe that you value yourself and your well-being. This not only sustains your creativity and productivity but also signals that you are ready to receive abundance and success. Remember, a well-cared-for author is a powerful magnet for their dreams and goals. So, treat yourself with kindness and watch as the Universe responds in kind.

Tips for Self-Care

- Set Boundaries: Designate specific times for writing and rest. Avoid burnout by balancing your schedule with activities that recharge you.

- Healthy Habits: Incorporate regular exercise, healthy eating, and sufficient sleep into your routine. A healthy body supports a creative mind.

- Mindfulness Practices: Engage in mindfulness or meditation to reduce stress and enhance focus. Even a few minutes a day can make a significant difference.

- Reflect and Appreciate: Keep a journal of the progress you've made. Reflecting on these achievements can boost your confidence and motivation.

Self-Care for Authors

One particular week, I was knee-deep in manuscript revisions and feeling the weight of deadlines looming over me. I hadn't taken a break in days, and my usual upbeat self was starting to resemble a grumpy cat who missed its afternoon nap. I knew I needed self-care before I hit burnout.

I decided to take a step back and treat myself to a "me" day. I indulged in my favorite cupcakes (guilt-free), and spent the afternoon binge-watching my favorite shows and spending time with my family and furbabies. That night, I even took a luxurious bubble bath with a book that had nothing to do with my genre. It was blissful.

The next day, I felt rejuvenated and more hopeful than ever. The break not only recharged my batteries but also gave me fresh perspectives on my work.

Reflecting on that experience, I realized the immense value of self-care. It wasn't just about the physical rest but about honoring myself and the efforts I put in every day. It taught me that taking care of myself was not a luxury but a necessity for my mental health. And those cupcakes? They tasted even sweeter knowing I had earned them.

Integrating self-care into your routine will not only improve your well-being but also reinforce your commitment to your writing goals. I recommend that you treat yourself with kindness and take breaks when needed; your future self will thank you.

29

Dare to Dream Big

The Successful Author dares to dream big and doesn't stress the opinions of others. In the world of writing, having a grand vision for your career is crucial. The Successful Author understands that to achieve greatness, you must first imagine it vividly. This means setting lofty goals, like becoming a bestselling author or winning prestigious literary awards, and believing in your ability to reach them. Dreaming big fuels your passion and gives you a clear direction to work towards, making the daily grind of writing more purposeful and rewarding.

However, with big dreams often comes a barrage of opinions from others—some supportive, but many critical or skeptical. And while feedback can be valuable, it's essential to filter out the noise and stay true to your vision. Worrying about what others think can stifle your creativity and derail your progress. Instead, I recommend focusing on your own goals and own inner guidance, understanding that true success comes from within.

Attempt to trust in yourself and disregard naysayers, and you will maintain the confidence and determination to succeed in life at whatever you set your mind to.

Tips for Daring to Dream Big

- Set Bold Goals: Don't be afraid to aim high. Define what success looks like for you and visualize it regularly.

- Stay True to Your Vision: Keep your big dreams at the forefront of your mind and let them guide your decisions, regardless of external opinions.

- Filter Feedback: Seek constructive criticism from trusted sources but learn to disregard unhelpful or negative comments.

- Trust Yourself: Cultivate a strong sense of self-belief and trust in your abilities and instincts.

- Surround Yourself with Positivity: Build a supportive network of fellow authors and achievers who encourage and inspire you.

Dare to Dream Big

Years and years ago, I announced to my friends and family that I was going to write a novel that would become a bestseller. The reactions were mixed, to say the least. Some were enthusiastic and supportive, while others gave me that polite, skeptical nod—the kind you give someone who just declared they're going to build a rocket ship in their backyard. I could practically hear the "Bless her heart" thoughts ringing in the air.

For a moment, I even doubted myself. Was I being unrealistic? But then, I decided to be my inner Successful Author and dream big anyway. I set a bold goal: to draft a novel that would not only be published but also be successful. I ignored the dubious looks and focused on my writing, pouring my heart and soul into every page.

Of course, there were times when the doubts crept in, usually after I'd spent an hour on social media comparing myself to other writers. But I learned to tune out the noise. I started each day with a visualization of my dream—seeing my book on bestseller lists, imagining the emails from ecstatic readers, and yes, visualizing the celebratory cupcakes I'd indulge in when I made it.

After months of hard work, I finally finished my manuscript. Despite the initial doubts from others, I sent it off to agents and publishers. The day I received my first acceptance letter from a publisher was surreal. I could almost hear those cynical voices being drowned out by my own cheers of joy. Unfortunately, that book did not become a *New York Times* bestseller.

And when many years later one of my self-published books eventually did hit the bestseller list, the feeling of accomplishment was indescribable.

This experience taught me that daring to dream big, never giving up, and ignoring the opinions of others is not just about reaching a goal; it's about believing in yourself and your vision. It reinforced the idea that success is often about persistence, self-belief, and the courage to dream beyond the ordinary.

So, dare to dream big, trust your instincts, and remember, the opinions of others are just that—opinions, not your reality.

30

Launch Plans, Schedules, and Marketing

THE SUCCESSFUL AUTHOR understands that writing a book is only the beginning. To truly thrive in the competitive world of publishing, it's essential to have a well-thought-out launch plan, a consistent publishing schedule, and effective marketing plans tailored to your target readership. A launch plan sets the stage for your book's debut, outlining the steps you'll take to build anticipation and maximize sales. It includes everything from setting a release date to planning promotional activities like blog tours, social media campaigns, and giveaways.

Equally important is maintaining a consistent publishing schedule. The Successful Author knows that regularly releasing new content keeps readers engaged and builds momentum. Whether it's a new book every few months or regular updates on a blog or social media, consistency helps to establish a reliable presence in your readers' lives.

Alongside this, understanding and effectively marketing to your target readership ensures that your efforts are reaching the right audience. This involves identifying who your readers are, what they enjoy, and where they spend their time online, then crafting messages and content that resonate with them.

Tips for Launch Planning, Scheduling, and Marketing

- Develop a Detailed Launch Plan: Include dates, promotional activities, and marketing strategies leading up to your book's release.

- Set a Realistic Publishing Schedule: Plan your writing and release dates in advance to maintain a steady flow of new content.

- Identify Your Target Audience: Understand the demographics, interests, and online behaviors of your ideal readers.

- Create Engaging Marketing Content: Tailor your promotional materials to appeal directly to your target audience.

- Utilize Multiple Platforms: Reach your readers through a mix of social media, email newsletters, and book promotion sites.

Launching, Schedules, Promoting

I remember when my debut novel was ready, I had no idea how to get it into the hands of readers. Enter the concept of a launch plan, a publishing schedule, and targeted marketing.

I started by creating a comprehensive launch plan. I set a release date and mapped out a countdown, complete with teaser posts, cover reveals, and even a book trailer. Next, I reached out to book bloggers and reviewers, set up a giveaway, and planned a virtual launch party.

Then I tackled my publishing schedule and I decided to release a new book every four months, a pace that kept me productive without feeling overwhelmed. I plotted out my writing time, set deadlines, and even factored in a few "cat-astrophe" days for when my feline friends inevitably caused a little mayhem.

Marketing was the final thing I needed to do. I dove into understanding my target audience—who they were, what genres they loved, and where they hung out online. Armed with this knowledge, I crafted engaging content that spoke directly to them. I joined reader groups, participated in Facebook group takeovers, and personalized my social media posts to spark interest and conversation.

The launch was a success, and I received wonderful feedback from readers who appreciated the effort I put into making the publication event special.

Through this experience, I learned the importance of planning, consistency, and understanding your audience. And most importantly, I realized that a little humor and flexibility go a long way as a successful author. I suggest you plan meticulously, market wisely, and never forget to enjoy your success.

31

Manifest Success and Wealth

THE SUCCESSFUL AUTHOR knows that manifesting success and prosperity is not just about hard work but also about cultivating the right mindset and using the principles of the law of attraction. So, let's discuss this topic again. I believe that by focusing on positive thoughts, visualizing success, and affirming abundance, the Successful Author effortlessly attracts prosperity and financial stability. This mindset shift can transform how you approach your writing career and open doors to opportunities you might not have thought possible.

Understanding and visualizing financial success is crucial to achieving it. Money provides security and comfort, allowing you to focus on your creative endeavors without the stress of financial instability. So, I suggest aligning your thoughts and actions with the energy of abundance, and you will set the stage for attracting more income and achieving your financial goals.

Tips for Manifesting Success and Money

- Visualize Abundance: Spend a few minutes each day visualizing financial success. Envision yourself receiving royalty checks, seeing your books on bestseller lists, and living comfortably.

- Affirmations: Use positive affirmations to reinforce your belief in your financial success. Statements like "I am a successful author" and "Money flows to me easily and effortlessly" can shift your mindset.

- Set Clear Financial Goals: Define specific financial goals and outline steps to achieve them. Whether it's hitting a certain sales number or earning a particular amount per month, clarity is necessary.

- Invest in Yourself: Don't be afraid to spend money on software, courses, and resources that can enhance your skills and boost your career. Investing in yourself is an investment in your future earnings.

- Gratitude: Cultivate an attitude of gratitude for the money you already have. Gratitude attracts more positive energy and abundance into your life.

Manifesting Money and Success

Talking about money tends to make people uncomfortable. I'm always in awe, a tad envious, and hugely inspired when I hear about indie authors killing it in the publishing world. I know many of you are like me, sometimes living payday to payday.

They say money can't buy happiness? I have to disagree! I sleep much better at night knowing my bills and rent are covered. Money provides security and comfort, and there's absolutely nothing wrong with that. Wanting to increase your income to live a better life isn't greedy; it's practical. After all, who wouldn't want a little financial peace of mind?

The day I decided to fully adopt the law of attraction to manifest financial success was during the time that I was inspired by several books on manifesting and attracting money. After reading each one, I started setting clear financial goals. I visualized the amount of money I needed to cover all my bills and rent, and then I took it a step further. I closed my eyes, feeling and imagining the relief and security that came with having my finances in order.

This soon became an inspiring ritual. My mindset started to shift. Instead of worrying about money, I began to feel more confident and empowered. I adopted a personal motto: "Where creativity flows, money follows." This became my truth. I love being a creative, a storyteller, and a book cover designer. I love having a job that I can do from home in my PJs. Although my co-workers (cute kitties) can be distracting, I am determined to become more successful going forward in my career.

The changes were almost immediate. Opportunities started to come my way—new clients for my design services, more book sales, and even unexpected financial windfalls. By focusing on abundance and maintaining a positive mindset, I was able to attract the financial success I had been seeking. My life, mindset, and author career improved dramatically. I now sleep better at night, knowing that my bills are paid and my financial future is secure.

I suggest you visualize your success and affirm your abundance. I believe that where creativity flows, money follows. Stay positive, establish specific goals, and watch as the Universe aligns to bring you the prosperity you deserve.

32

Successful Author's Morning Routine

THE SUCCESSFUL AUTHOR knows that the way they start their day can have a profound impact on their career. A well-crafted morning routine sets the tone for the entire day, inspiring a positive mindset, enhancing productivity, and ensuring that they approach their writing with clarity and focus. The first hours of the morning are crucial for aligning thoughts, setting intentions, and preparing both mentally and physically for a successful start.

An effective morning routine doesn't have to be complex or time-consuming. It's about creating a series of positive habits that ground you, inspire you, and prepare you for a productive day. This might include activities such as meditation, journaling, reading, exercise, or simply enjoying a quiet cup of coffee while visualizing your goals. The Successful Author understands that these morning rituals are not just about checking off tasks, but about cultivating a mindset that attracts success and creativity throughout the day.

Incorporating these practices into your morning routine can transform the way you approach your work. Start with a few minutes of meditation to clear your mind and set positive intentions for the day. Follow this with a brief journaling session where you can outline your goals and express gratitude, setting a tone of positivity and focus. Adding some physical activity, whether it's a short walk, yoga, or a quick workout, can energize your body and boost your mood.

Tips for a Successful Morning Routine

- Wake Up Early: Give yourself ample time to start the day without rushing. Early mornings are often quiet and free from distractions, making them ideal for setting the tone for the day.

- Meditate or Practice Mindfulness: Spend a few minutes in meditation or mindfulness practice to clear your mind and focus your intentions for the day.

- Journaling: Write down your thoughts, goals, and affirmations. This helps to set clear intentions and keep you passionate.

- Exercise: Incorporate some physical activity to boost your energy levels and improve your mood. Even a short walk can make a significant difference.

- Read or Listen to Something Inspirational: Start your

day with inspiration. Read a chapter from a motivational book or listen to an uplifting podcast.

- Plan Your Day: Outline your projects and priorities for the day. Having a clear plan helps you stay focused and productive.

The Power of a Good Morning Routine

A good morning routine transformed my writing career. It's early morning, and my house is still quiet. My cats are lazily stretching in their favorite spots, and I've just poured myself a steaming cup of vanilla and cinnamon coffee. I used to be a night owl, often writing late into the night and waking up feeling groggy and unfocused. But one day, I decided to shake things up and establish an earlier morning routine.

I started by setting my alarm for six am. The first few mornings were tough—my bed felt extra cozy, and I just wanted to keep hitting the snooze button. But I pushed through. I began each day with a few minutes of meditation, focusing on my breath and clearing my mind. This simple practice made a world of difference. I felt calmer and more centered.

Next, I incorporated journaling. I'd jot down my goals for the day, a few positive affirmations, and my gratitude list. One of my favorite affirmations was, "Today, creativity flows effortlessly, and words come easily." Writing it down each morning set a positive tone for my writing sessions.

Exercise was another crucial addition. Now, I'm not talking about a full-blown workout—just a quick 15-minute low impact aerobics or a brisk walk around the block. It woke me up and got my blood flowing, which was especially helpful for shaking off any lingering sleepiness.

I also made it a habit to read a chapter from an inspirational book while sipping my coffee. One morning, I was moved by a passage from a money manifesting guide which reminded me of the power of mindset in attracting abundance. Feeling inspired, I planned my day, listing my top priorities and setting a clear intention for my writing.

My productivity increased, and I felt more creative and encouraged than ever. I was able to write more consistently and with greater focus. The morning routine became a sacred time for me—a foundation that set the tone for a successful day.

Through this practice, I learned that the way you start your day truly matters. A good morning routine can transform your mindset, boost your productivity, and set you up for success. I encourage you to craft your own morning routine. Find what works for you, and make it a non-negotiable part of your day. Your future successful self will thank you.

33

Stress, Writer's Block, Low Self-Esteem

THE SUCCESSFUL AUTHOR knows that the writing journey can be fraught with challenges such as stress, writer's block, low self-esteem, and a lack of direction. These hurdles can feel overwhelming, but there are tangible and effective solutions to help you overcome them and keep moving forward. By employing these strategies, you can align yourself with the principles of the law of attraction and manifest a successful and fulfilling writing career.

When stress threatens to derail your progress, take a step back and practice mindfulness or meditation to regain your focus and calm your mind. To conquer writer's block, try changing your environment, setting smaller writing goals, or engaging in creative activities that spark inspiration. If low self-esteem is holding you back, affirmations and positive self-talk can help rebuild your confidence. And when you're feeling directionless, revisiting your goals and creating a clear action plan can provide the guidance you need.

Another effective strategy is to seek support from a community of fellow writers. The Successful Author knows that connecting with others who share similar goals and problems can provide valuable encouragement and insight. Join writing groups, attend workshops, or participate in online forums where you can share your experiences and learn from others.

Sometimes, just knowing you're not alone in your struggles can make a world of difference. Plus, mentors, life (author) coaches, and accountability partners can offer guidance and keep you on track.

I suggest staying aligned with your goals and the principles of the law of attraction

Tips for Overcoming Common Challenges

- Manage Stress: Incorporate mindfulness, meditation, or deep-breathing exercises into your daily routine to reduce stress and improve focus.

- Beat Writer's Block: Change your writing environment, set doable and more manageable writing goals, or take a break to engage in creative activities.

- Boost Self-Esteem: Use positive affirmations and self-talk to build confidence and remind yourself of your worth and capabilities.

- Find Direction: Revisit your goals and create a clear

action plan with specific, easy steps to guide your progress.

Conquering Writer's Block and Stress

One cold wintery day, I found myself staring blankly at my screen. Writer's block had hit me hard, and the stress of looming deadlines was making it worse. My self-esteem was taking a nosedive, and I felt utterly directionless.

In a moment of frustration, I recalled the principles of the law of attraction and decided to put them into practice. To start with, I knew I had to tackle the stress. I did a short meditation session every morning for a month. Sitting cross-legged on the floor, I began to meditate on my anxiety and blockages, sometimes with a cat curled up on my lap. Surprisingly, these moments began to calm my mind and reduce my stress levels.

Soon after that, I addressed the writer's block. I changed my writing environment by moving my desk to a different part of the room. This minor change made a big difference. I also set writing goals—rather than aiming for a full chapter, I focused on writing every day without a word count in mind. This helped me regain my momentum.

To perk up my self-esteem, I started using positive affirmations. Every morning, I would look in the mirror and say, "I am a successful author, and I attract new readers daily." Initially, it felt like a bit of a lie, yet over time, I noticed a change in my confidence.

Finally, to find direction, I revisited my goals and created a clear action plan. I broke down my larger goals into specific, achievable steps and created a timeline for each. This gave me a sense of direction and purpose, and the stress melted away.

My stress levels decreased, my writer's block vanished, and my confidence returned. I was back on track and more productive than ever. This experience taught me that the Successful Author doesn't shy away from obstacles but tackles each one with practical solutions and a positive mindset.

So, if you're ever struggling with stress, writer's block, low self-esteem, or a lack of direction, remember that you have the power to overcome these issues. Apply these tips, do your best to stay positive, and watch as your writing career levels up. And if all else fails, try meditating with a furbaby on your lap—it worked wonders for me.

34

Frequency and High Vibrations to Manifest Success

THE SUCCESSFUL AUTHOR knows that maintaining a high frequency and positive vibrations is key to manifesting success, bestseller status, and increased book sales. According to the law of attraction, like attracts like. This means that by raising your energy and maintaining an optimistic mindset, you can attract the success and abundance you desire. The energy you put out into the world is what you receive in return.

One way to raise your frequency is by engaging in activities that make you feel happy and inspired. This could be anything from spending time in nature, practicing gratitude, or indulging in a creative hobby. The Successful Author also understands the importance of surrounding themselves with positivity, whether that's through uplifting music, inspiring books, or supportive friends and colleagues. High vibrations not only enhance your mood but also enhance your creativity and productivity.

I suggest actively managing your thoughts and emotions to stay aligned with your ambitions. This involves letting go of negative self-talk and replacing it with positive affirmations. By visualizing your desired outcomes and feeling the emotions associated with those achievements, you align your vibration with success. Remember, the Universe responds to the energy you emit, so keeping your frequency high is essential for manifesting your dreams.

Also, the Successful Author recognizes that the Universe responds not only to your thoughts and feelings but also to your actions. Consistently taking inspired action towards your goals, no matter how small, signals to the Universe that you are committed and ready to receive the success you seek. This means showing up for your writing sessions, engaging with your readers, and continually improving your craft.

I recommend aligning your actions with your high-frequency mindset, and you will create a powerful synergy that propels you in the direction of your dreams. The Universe rewards this alignment by presenting you with opportunities, ideas, and connections that help you succeed, reinforcing the positive cycle of manifestation.

Tips for Raising Your Frequency and Aligning with High Vibrations

- Engage in Pleasurable Activities: Spend time doing things that bring you happiness and inspiration. This will elevate your mood and energy levels.

- Practice Gratitude: Regularly acknowledge and appreciate the good things in your life. Gratitude raises your vibration and attracts more positivity.

- Surround Yourself with Positivity: Listen to uplifting music, read inspiring books, and connect with supportive people who encourage and cheer on your career.

- Use Positive Affirmations: Replace negative thoughts with empowering statements that reinforce your belief in your success.

- Visualize Your Success: Imagine your goals as already achieved. Feel the emotions of accomplishment and let this positive energy wash over you.

- Acts of Kindness: Acts of kindness towards others raise your vibration and create a positive ripple effect.

- Stay Excited and Passionate: Keep your passion for writing alive by setting exciting goals and rejoicing in your accomplishments.

- Focus on the Present Moment: Stay present and mindful, appreciating each moment and the progress you're making.

Raising My Frequency for Success

I'll tell you how I raised my frequency to manifest greater success in my writing career. A few years ago, my sales were at an all-time low, and I felt discouraged. It was one of those times when I questioned why I ever thought becoming a full-time author was a good idea. But then I became determined to take a proactive approach to shift my energy.

I started by incorporating more gratitude into my daily routine. (*I know I talk a lot about gratitude, but it really is a powerful way to manifest success quicker!*) Every morning, after my usual coffee and Greek yogurt (because let's be honest, caffeine and a healthy breakfast are non-negotiable), I made it a point to reflect on things I was genuinely grateful for. I began each day with a short walk in the park, soaking in the beauty of nature and feeling grateful for the fresh air and the serene environment. This simple change lifted my spirits and set a positive tone for the day.

Gradually, I noticed a shift. My mood improved, and the grateful energy that I put into my writing was different—more vibrant and enthusiastic. And then, something incredible happened. My sales started to pick up, and I made more money that month than I had all year. It was as if the Universe had been waiting for me to align my energy with my goals. Gratitude, it turns out, wasn't just good manners—it was a powerful magnet for success.

This experience taught me that raising your frequency and maintaining high vibrations is crucial for manifesting success. I suggest focusing on positivity, gratitude, and happiness, so you can attract the success you desire and deserve. Take the time to elevate your energy and watch as the Universe responds in kind.

Authentic Author Self to Align with Your Desires

THE SUCCESSFUL AUTHOR knows that uncovering their authentic self is crucial to manifesting success, happiness, and becoming a full-time author. Authenticity is about embracing who you truly are, including your strengths, weaknesses, passions, and unique voice. By aligning with your true self, you attract opportunities that resonate with your desires and create a fulfilling writing career.

When you uncover your authentic self, you align your actions with your deepest desires, making the road to success smoother and more enjoyable. The Successful Author understands that authenticity builds trust with readers, creating a loyal fanbase that values your genuine voice. This alignment not only enhances your creativity but also brings joy and satisfaction to your work, making the journey towards becoming a full-time author more rewarding.

I suggest aligning with your desires and being clear about what you want to achieve and why. The Successful Author sets goals that reflect their true aspirations, not just what they think they should do. This clarity helps you stay driven and inspired, ensuring that your efforts are directed towards what truly matters to you. I recommend living authentically and pursuing your genuine desires, so you will attract the success and happiness you seek.

Also, the law of attraction teaches that the Universe responds to the energy you project. When you are authentic, your energy is pure and aligned with your true self, making it easier for the Universe to respond positively. The Successful Author knows that when you embrace your authentic self, you send out a clear signal that attracts opportunities, connections, and resources that are in harmony with your goals. This genuine alignment ensures that the success you manifest is not only attainable but also deeply satisfying. So, be true to yourself, and create a magnetic pull that brings your dreams into reality, effortlessly guiding you towards a fulfilling and prosperous writing career.

Ways to Uncover Your Authentic Self

- Focus on Your True Passions: Take time to explore what truly excites and motivates you. Write down your passions and interests to gain clarity.

- Appreciate Your Unique Voice: Be confident in your individuality and let your true self shine through in your writing.

- Set Authentic Goals: Align your goals with your genuine desires, ensuring they reflect what you truly want to achieve.

- Practice Self-Compassion: Accept and embrace your imperfections. Authenticity includes being kind to yourself and recognizing your worth.

- Stay True to Your Values: Let your personal values guide your decisions and actions, creating a strong foundation for your career.

Embracing My Authentic Self

When I first started writing, I was struggling to find my voice as an author. I was trying to write in a style that didn't feel true to me because I thought it was what readers wanted. The result? My work felt forced, and I was constantly stressed and unhappy.

One day, I resolved to change my approach. I sat down and reflected on what truly excited me about writing. I asked myself what stories I loved to tell and what messages I wanted to share with the world. I realized that my true passion lay in writing novels with strong, quirky characters, romance, mysteries, and unexpected plot twists. It was a far cry from the serious literary fiction I had been attempting to write.

So, I took a leap of faith and started writing the kind of stories that made my heart happy. At first, it was terrifying. I worried that no one would read my work or that I would be judged for my unconventional style. But as I continued to write authentically, something amazing happened. I began to enjoy writing again. My creativity flourished, and the words flowed effortlessly.

Aligning with my true desires also helped me set authentic goals. Instead of aiming for what I thought was expected, I focused on what I genuinely wanted to achieve. This shift in mindset made a huge difference. I felt more confident and inspired, and my work resonated more deeply with readers. My audience grew, and I started receiving heartfelt messages from fans who appreciated my unique voice.

Through this experience, I learned that uncovering your authentic self and aligning with your desires is essential for success and happiness.

I suggest that you give your authentic self a hug and let your true desires guide you. The journey to becoming a full-time author will be much more rewarding and enjoyable. And who knows? You might just find that your true self is exactly what the world of books has been waiting for.

Successful Author Wrap-Up

THE SUCCESSFUL AUTHOR understands that the mindset they cultivate is just as crucial as the words they write. By embracing the principles of the law of attraction, they harness the power of positive thinking, visualization, and intentional action to manifest their dreams. This approach isn't about wishful thinking or passive hoping; it's about actively creating the conditions for success through focused mental and emotional practices. The Successful Author knows that their thoughts and feelings are remarkable ways to shape their reality, influencing both their creative output and the opportunities that come their way.

At the heart of this philosophy is the idea that *like* attracts *like*. The Successful Author realizes that by maintaining a positive outlook and focusing on their goals, they can attract positive experiences and outcomes. This means consistently aligning their thoughts, words, and actions with their deepest desires. Whether it's visualizing their book hitting the bestseller list, setting clear and achievable goals, or maintaining a gratitude practice, they know that these habits build a strong foundation for success. The law of attraction teaches that what you focus on expands, so be diligent about directing your focus toward what you want to achieve.

Moreover, recognize the importance of taking inspired action. They understand that while the law of attraction emphasizes the power of mindset, it also requires active participation in their business. This means not only dreaming big but also putting in the effort to make those dreams a reality.

By combining a positive mindset with practical steps and a commitment to following your dreams, you will create a dynamic and proactive approach to your career. This constructive collaboration of belief and action propels the Successful Author forward, opening doors and attracting the right opportunities to support their success.

35 Inspiring Ways to be a Successful Author Recap

- Visualize Your Success: Spend a few minutes each day visualizing your ultimate goals. See yourself signing books, receiving accolades, and enjoying the success you desire. The clearer your vision, the more powerfully you attract it.

- Set Clear Intentions: Be specific about what you want to achieve. Write down your goals and revisit them regularly. Clarity of purpose aligns your actions with your desires.

- Positive Affirmations: Use affirmations to reinforce your belief in your abilities. Statements like "I am a successful author" or "My books earn money and captivate readers" can help shift your mindset towards success.

- Gratitude Practice: Start each day by listing things you are grateful for. Gratitude shifts your focus from what you lack to the abundance you already have, attracting more positive experiences into your life.

- Surround Yourself with Positivity: Engage with supportive and like-minded individuals. Join writing groups, attend workshops, and network with other authors who inspire and uplift you.

- Take Inspired Action: The law of attraction is not just about thinking and feeling; it's also about doing. Take concrete steps towards your goals, even if they are minor. Action amplifies your intentions.

- Stay Persistent and Patient: Success doesn't happen overnight. Keep your focus and remain patient. Trust that your efforts will pay off in due time.

- Eliminate Negative Self-Talk: Be mindful of your inner dialogue. Replace negative thoughts with positive ones. Instead of thinking, "I'll never finish this book," tell yourself, "I am making steady progress every day."

- Create a Vision Board: Fill a board with images and words that represent your goals and dreams. Place it where you can see it daily and use it as a reminder of your dreams.

- Award Yourself: Acknowledge and celebrate each milestone, no matter how small. This builds momentum and reinforces your progress.

- Maintain a Growth Mindset: Face all challenges with a positive mindset and learn from your failures. Viewing obstacles as opportunities for growth keeps you resilient and impassioned.

- Stay Open to Opportunities: Be open to new ideas and opportunities. Sometimes, success comes from unexpected places. Stay flexible and ready to adapt.

- Align Your Environment: Ensure your workspace and surroundings reflect your goals. A tidy, inspiring space can significantly impact your productivity and creativity.

By incorporating these law of attraction-based tips into your daily routine, you will create a positive and proactive approach to achieving your writing goals. Be conscious of the energy you put out into the world is the energy you attract back, so stay positive, stay focused, and believe in your success.

The Law of Attraction Author

Let me tell you about the time I decided to take the law of attraction seriously in my writing career. It's Monday morning, my coffee is still too hot to drink, and my cats are in a conspiracy to keep me from my laptop by using it as their personal sleeping space. I was feeling like my writing career was going nowhere. So, I decided to try this whole "positive thinking" and "visualization" thing. After all, what did I have to lose besides my mind?

I started with a vision board. I grabbed some old magazines, a pair of scissors, and a glue stick that my daughter had left behind from her last school project. The cats watched in fascination (or perhaps judgment) as I cut out pictures of book covers, bestseller lists, and author signing events. I even added a photo of a ridiculously oversized cupcake to represent the sweet taste of success.

Every morning, I would sip my sweetened coffee and spend a few minutes staring at my vision board, imagining myself in those pictures. I figured that at the very least, it was better than starting my day by doomscrolling through social media.

Then, I moved on to positive affirmations. At first, saying things like "I am a successful author" and "My books sell millions" felt a bit like I was auditioning for a part in a cheesy motivational infomercial. But, with my cats as my reluctant audience, I persisted. And do you know what? Slowly but surely, something shifted. I started to believe my own words. My writing sessions became more productive, and I found myself genuinely excited about my projects.

Then one day, I checked my email and saw an influx of messages from writers thanking me for my new nonfiction series, which had reached thousands and was changing lives. Writers shared heartfelt stories of how my advice had reignited their passion for writing, helped them overcome creative blocks, and provided them with the tools they needed to achieve their dreams. Some even credited the series with giving them the confidence to publish their first book or take their author business to the next level. It was overwhelming and incredibly gratifying to see the tangible impact my work was having on so many lives. Teary-eyed, I nearly choked on my celebratory cupcake, feeling a profound sense of accomplishment and gratitude for being able to contribute to the writing community in such a meaningful way.

Looking back, I realize that embracing the law of attraction helped me transform my mindset and my career. By focusing on positive outcomes and visualizing my success, I not only changed my outlook but also opened myself up to living my very best writing life. The experience taught me that a little bit of positive thinking, combined with a lot of determination (and maybe some cat hair on my work PJs), can go a long way.

To all the writers out there: dare to dream big, believe in your potential, and don't forget to enjoy the victories—complete with coffee, cats, and cupcakes.

Successful Author Affirmations

HERE ARE 25 positive affirmations to inspire and motivate you to achieve author career success:

1. I am a successful and accomplished author.

2. My words inspire and captivate readers around the world.

3. Every day, my writing improves and my creativity flows effortlessly.

4. I attract opportunities for my books to reach a wider audience.

5. My books are bestsellers and beloved by readers.

6. I am confident in my abilities and my unique voice.

7. My writing career is flourishing and growing every day.

8. I am dedicated to my craft and committed to my success.

9. Positive energy surrounds my writing and my career.

10. I am grateful for the success and recognition my books receive.

11. My stories have a profound impact on those who read them.

12. I am disciplined and focused in my writing routine.

13. I attract supportive readers, industry professionals, and fellow authors.

14. My books receive glowing reviews and accolades.

15. I am constantly learning and growing as a writer.

16. My creativity is boundless and my ideas are limitless.

17. I am proud of my accomplishments and excited for my future.

18. Writing brings me joy, fulfillment, and financial abundance.

19. I am resilient and persistent in the face of challenges.

20. My writing career is a source of pride and inspiration for others.

21. I am open to new opportunities and experiences in my author business.

22. My books are a reflection of my passion and dedication.

23. I am a magnet for success, prosperity, and happiness.

24. I am confident in my ability to achieve all my writing goals.

25. I am so thankful to be living my dream as a successful author.

38

Affirmations for Manifesting Money and Increasing Book Sales

HERE ARE positive affirmations to help you manifest money and increase your book sales:

1. Money flows effortlessly and abundantly into my life.

2. My books are highly sought after and sell rapidly.

3. I am open to receiving financial abundance from my writing.

4. Every day, my book sales increase and my income grows.

5. I attract readers who love and support my work.

6. My writing is valuable and people are eager to pay for it.

7. I am deserving of financial success and prosperity.

8. My books are bestsellers and consistently generate income.

9. I am grateful for the financial abundance my writing brings me.

10. My marketing efforts are effective and boost my book sales.

11. Opportunities to earn money from my books come to me easily.

12. My income from book sales continues to grow exponentially.

13. I am a successful author with a thriving financial life.

14. My financial goals are within reach and I achieve them effortlessly.

15. I attract book influencers and have successful book promotions.

16. My books are entertaining and people are happy to buy them.

17. I am confident in my ability to generate significant income from my writing.

18. My creativity leads to financial abundance and success.

19. I am a magnet for wealth and prosperity through my writing.

20. My book sales are consistent and steadily increasing.

21. I manifest money with ease and my bank account reflects my success.

22. Readers are excited to purchase my books and share them with others.

23. I am financially secure and my writing career is thriving.

24. I attract wealth and abundance through my published works.

25. My books are in high demand and my financial rewards are endless.

39

Affirmations to Attract More readers

HERE ARE positive affirmations to help you attract new readers and superfans who love your work:

1. I attract new readers who are excited to discover my books.

2. My writing resonates deeply with readers and creates superfans.

3. Every day, more people are drawn to my stories and my voice.

4. My books reach the perfect audience who loves and appreciates them.

5. I am surrounded by loyal superfans who eagerly await my next release.

6. New readers find my books and instantly become captivated.

7. My stories inspire a dedicated and enthusiastic fanbase.

8. I am grateful for the readers who support and promote my work.

9. My writing attracts a growing community of engaged readers.

10. I create stories that turn readers into lifelong superfans.

11. My readers connect with my characters and themes on a deep level.

12. I am a magnet for readers who love and cherish my books.

13. Word of mouth spreads, bringing new readers to my stories.

14. My books are recommended and shared by passionate readers.

15. I attract readers who feel a personal connection to my work.

16. My superfans are excited to share my books with others.

17. I cultivate a vibrant and supportive reader community.

18. My writing inspires loyalty and admiration from my readers.

19. Every book I release attracts more superfans who love my work.

20. My readers eagerly anticipate and pre-order my new releases.

21. I am surrounded by readers who appreciate and celebrate my creativity.

22. My stories touch the hearts of readers and turn them into superfans.

23. I attract a diverse audience who finds joy in my writing.

24. My books create lasting impressions and memorable experiences for readers.

25. I am thankful for the readers who passionately support my writing journey.

40

Affirmations to Become Positive and Empowered

HERE ARE positive affirmations to help you banish negativity and become a more positive, empowered author:

1. I release all negativity and believe in positivity in my writing career.

2. I am a confident and empowered author, free from self-doubt.

3. My mind is filled with positive thoughts that fuel my creativity.

4. I attract only positive energy and supportive people into my life.

5. I am resilient and overcome any challenges with grace and confidence.

6. I believe in my abilities and trust in my unique voice as a writer.

7. I am surrounded by positivity, inspiration, and encouragement.

8. Negative thoughts have no power over me; I choose positivity.

9. I am in control of my emotions and focus on the positive aspects of my life.

10. I am grateful for my talents and for being able to do my dream job.

11. I create my reality with positive thinking and empowered actions.

12. I am worthy of success and accept my achievements with pride.

13. I let go of fear and welcome new opportunities with open arms.

14. My positive attitude attracts success, joy, and fulfillment.

15. I am strong, confident, and capable of achieving my goals.

16. I focus on my strengths and celebrate my progress every day.

17. I am surrounded by a community of supportive and uplifting individuals.

18. I choose to see the good in every situation and learn from every experience.

19. I am a beacon of positivity and empowerment in the writing community.

20. I trust the Universe and know that every step brings me closer to my dreams.

21. I am resilient and bounce back from setbacks stronger than before.

22. I radiate positivity, attracting abundance and success into my life.

23. I am an empowered author who writes with passion and purpose.

24. I let go of past mistakes and focus on the limitless possibilities ahead.

25. I am a positive force in the world, and my writing reflects my inner strength and joy.

41

Affirmations on Goals and a Positive Mindset

HERE ARE positive affirmations focused on achieving goals and maintaining a positive mindset:

1. I am focused and determined to achieve my goals.

2. My mindset is positive and geared towards success.

3. I accomplish everything I set my mind to.

4. I attract success and prosperity into my life.

5. My goals are within reach, and I am capable of achieving them.

6. Positive thoughts drive my actions towards success.

7. I believe in myself and my ability to achieve my dreams.

8. Each day, I move closer to achieving my goals.

9. I am confident in my skills and talents.

10. I think positively and expect the best outcomes.

11. I am proactive and take steps to achieve my goals.

12. My mind is clear, focused, and ready for success.

13. I am persistent and never give up on my goals.

14. Positive energy surrounds me and fuels my ambition.

15. I am capable of achieving greatness.

16. My positive mindset attracts opportunities for success.

17. I set clear goals and work towards them with confidence.

18. I am a goal-oriented person who achieves what I set out to do.

19. My thoughts are positive, and they create my reality.

20. I am successful in everything I do.

21. I am driven, motivated, and always moving forward.

22. I attract success through my positive attitude and hard work.

23. I am clear about my goals and confident in my abilities.

24. My positive mindset brings me closer to my dreams every day.

25. I am committed to achieving my goals and living my best life.

42

Affirmations to Boost Confidence

HERE ARE positive affirmations to boost confidence in your author career and writing:

1. I am a talented and confident writer.

2. My words have power and affect readers deeply.

3. I trust in my creative abilities and unique voice.

4. My writing is valuable and deserves to be read.

5. I am proud of my accomplishments as an author.

6. I am fearless in sharing my stories with the world.

7. My confidence grows with each word I write.

8. I am a successful and positive author.

9. My writing is a gift that I share confidently.

10. I believe in my talent and potential as a writer.

11. I write with assurance and conviction.

12. My stories resonate with readers and leave a lasting impression.

13. I am confident in my ability to create compelling narratives.

14. My writing process flows smoothly and effortlessly.

15. I have faith in my skills and my future as an author.

16. My work is appreciated and admired by my readers.

17. I am bold and daring in my creative endeavors.

18. My confidence shines through in every piece I write.

19. I am worthy of success and recognition as an author.

20. I am courageous in exploring new ideas and themes.

21. My writing is a reflection of my confident and authentic self.

22. I inspire others with my confident storytelling.

23. I am resilient and confident in the face of challenges.

24. My confidence attracts opportunities for growth and success.

25. I am a confident and influential voice in the literary world.

43

Affirmations on Gratitude

HERE ARE gratitude affirmations on writing, money, and author success:

1. I am grateful for my creative talents and the ability to write.

2. I am thankful for the success I have achieved as an author.

3. I appreciate the financial abundance my writing brings me.

4. I am grateful for my loyal readers and their support.

5. I am thankful for the opportunities to share my stories with the world.

6. I appreciate the positive feedback and reviews from my readers.

7. I am grateful for the inspiration that flows effortlessly into my writing.

8. I am thankful for the financial security my writing career provides.

9. I appreciate the growth and progress I make with each writing project.

10. I am grateful for the joy and fulfillment writing brings into my life.

11. I am thankful for the connections I make with other writers and readers.

12. I appreciate the recognition and accolades my work receives.

13. I am grateful for the financial rewards of my successful author career.

14. I am thankful for the creative ideas that come to me easily.

15. I appreciate the support and encouragement from my writing community.

16. I am grateful for the discipline and dedication I have to my craft.

17. I am thankful for the freedom and flexibility my writing career offers.

18. I appreciate the positive influence my writing has on others.

19. I am grateful for the opportunities to grow and improve as a writer.

20. I am thankful for the financial success that allows me to live comfortably.

21. I appreciate the satisfaction of completing my writing projects.

22. I am grateful for the inspiration that helps me create compelling stories.

23. I am thankful for the financial abundance that supports my creative endeavors.

24. I appreciate the joy of seeing my books in the hands of readers.

25. I am grateful for the recognition and respect I receive as an author.

26. I am thankful for the steady stream of income from my book sales.

27. I appreciate the ability to share my passion for writing with the world.

28. I am grateful for the positive influence my writing has on my readers.

29. I am thankful for the financial freedom my successful writing career provides.

30. I appreciate the continuous flow of creativity and inspiration in my life.

44

Clearing and Energizing Affirmations for Money and Abundance

HERE ARE CLEARING and energizing affirmations for writers focusing on money and abundance:

1. I am worthy of financial abundance through my writing.

2. Money flows effortlessly to me as I pursue my passion for writing.

3. I attract lucrative opportunities and successful book deals.

4. My writing brings me joy and financial prosperity.

5. I am a magnet for wealth and abundance.

6. My books are bestsellers, and they generate substantial income.

7. I am open to receiving unexpected financial blessings.

8. I am grateful for the financial success my writing career provides.

9. I consistently earn more money from my writing every day.

10. I am financially rewarded for my creativity and hard work.

11. Abundance and prosperity are my birthright as a successful author.

12. My writing income allows me to live comfortably and securely.

13. I attract readers who love my work and support my financial growth.

14. Every word I write brings me closer to financial freedom.

15. I am confident in my ability to generate wealth through my writing.

16. My writing talent opens doors to unlimited financial opportunities.

17. I am prosperous and successful in all my writing endeavors.

18. My books provide immense value and are eagerly purchased by readers.

19. I am surrounded by supportive people who contribute to my financial success.

20. I am aligned with the energy of abundance, and it flows to me with ease.

45

Affirmations to Harness Your Intuition and Divine Energy

HERE ARE positive affirmations for writers to harness intuition and divine energy to unlock their potential:

1. I trust my intuition to guide me in my writing journey.

2. Divine energy flows through me, inspiring every word I write.

3. My creative potential is limitless and always accessible.

4. I am in tune with my inner wisdom and creative spirit.

5. I harness divine inspiration to create meaningful and impactful stories.

6. My intuition leads me to write authentically and powerfully.

7. I am open to receiving divine guidance for my writing.

8. My creative energy is a gift from the Universe, and I use it wisely.

9. I trust the process and know that my intuition will never lead me astray.

10. My writing is a reflection of my highest self and divine purpose.

11. I am connected to a higher source of inspiration and creativity.

12. I listen to my inner voice and follow its guidance in my writing.

13. My intuition helps me create stories that resonate deeply with readers.

14. Divine energy flows effortlessly through me, unlocking my full potential.

15. I am a channel for divine creativity and wisdom.

16. I trust that my intuition will lead me to success and fulfillment in my writing career.

17. My intuition and divine energy guide me to write with clarity and purpose.

18. I am aligned with the Universe, and my writing reflects this harmony.

19. I honor my intuitive insights and allow them to shape my writing.

20. My writing is a powerful expression of my divine connection and inner truth.

46

Positive Affirmations for the Universe

HERE ARE positive affirmations for writers to attract success and improve finances:

1. I am a successful author, and my books are in high demand.

2. The Universe supports my writing career and financial growth.

3. I effortlessly attract opportunities that enhance my success as an author.

4. My writing generates substantial and consistent income.

5. I am open to receiving financial abundance from my creative work.

6. The Universe aligns to bring me success and prosperity as a writer.

7. My books sell easily, and I am financially rewarded for my talent.

8. I am grateful for the financial success my writing career provides.

9. I attract wealth and abundance through my writing endeavors.

10. The Universe guides me to make wise financial decisions for my writing career.

11. My words have power, and they attract success and prosperity.

12. I am confident in my ability to achieve financial success as an author.

13. I am a magnet for financial abundance and successful opportunities.

14. My writing brings joy to readers and prosperity to my life.

15. The Universe is conspiring in my favor to enhance my writing career.

16. I trust that my financial needs are met with ease and grace.

17. I am open to receiving unexpected financial blessings through my writing.

18. My creative energy attracts wealth and success effortlessly.

19. I am financially secure and thriving as a successful author.

20. The Universe continually provides me with opportunities to grow my income through writing.

47

Conclusion

As you close this guide, keep in mind that becoming a successful author is uniquely yours. Embracing the principles of the law of attraction can transform not only your career but also your life. It's about harnessing the power of positive thinking, visualization, and intentional action to create the success you desire. Every step you take, no matter how small, brings you closer to your dreams. Believe in yourself, trust the process, and know that you are capable of achieving greatness.

It's important to stay resilient and maintain a positive mindset even when things get tough. Surround yourself with supportive people who believe in your vision, and don't be afraid to seek out inspiration from others. The law of attraction teaches us that we attract what we focus on, so keep your thoughts and intentions aligned with your highest aspirations.

And don't forget to celebrate your progress and successes. Each word written, each book published, and each reader touched by your work is a testament to your dedication and passion. Recognize the lessons learned from both your successes and setbacks, as they are all part of your growth as a writer. Stay committed to your goals, and don't let fear or doubt hold you back. The Universe is always listening, ready to support you in manifesting your dreams.

Finally, always keep your heart open to new possibilities and your mind attuned to the abundance that surrounds you. Trust in your creative abilities and the unique stories you have to share. You are a powerful creator, capable of manifesting a successful and fulfilling author career. Let your passion guide you, your persistence drive you, and your positive mindset empower you.

Here's to your continued success, inspired by the boundless potential within you. I believe in you—you got this!

Review Request

HEY THERE, future Successful Author,

Thank you so much for reading this guide to manifesting your writing dreams. I hope you found the tips, stories, and insights in this book as inspiring and empowering as I did while putting them together.

If you enjoyed this guide and found it helpful, I would be incredibly grateful if you could take a few moments to leave a review. Your feedback not only helps other writers discover the book, but also keeps the positive energy flowing in our amazing writing community.

Plus, I'd love to hear your thoughts and see how these tips have helped you on your way to becoming a successful author.

Happy writing and may all your dreams come true!

With gratitude,

S. A. Soule

Fiction Writing Tools

Each of these helpful and inexpensive self-editing books in the *Fiction Writing Tools* series encompass many different topics such as, dialogue, exposition, internal-monologue, setting, and other editing techniques that will help you take your writing skills to the next level.

THE WRITER'S GUIDE TO CHARACTER EMOTION

Most writers struggle with drafting a captivating story. The fastest way to take your writing to the next level is by the use of "deep Point-of-View" which can transform any novel from mediocre storytelling into riveting prose. This manual will explain how you can greatly enhance your characterization, and how to emerge your readers so deeply into a scene that they'll experience the story along with your characters. Also, learn how to avoid "telling" by applying "showing" methods through powerful examples that will deepen the reader's experience through vivid, sensory details.

THE WRITER'S GUIDE TO CHARACTER EXPRESSION

Fastest Way to Improve Dialogue, Settings, and Characterization

No matter what genre you write, this second manual on the deep Point of View technique should be kept as a vital reference in every writer's toolbox. This in-depth guide offers specific, practical tools for creative fiction writers on how to use the deep POV method to create realistic settings, visceral responses, and lifelike characters.

Crammed with even more examples and ways to eliminate shallow writing, this book also gives writers invaluable techniques required to master describing facial expressions, body language, "voice," and character emotions. This helpful source of endless inspiration will instantly enhance the reader's experience by explaining how to *dig deeper* to "show don't tell," which is necessary to crafting compelling dialogue, vivid scenes, and deepening characterization.

THE WRITER'S GUIDE TO VIVID SETTINGS AND CHARACTERS

Learn to Create a Realistic Setting with Atmospheric Detail and Lifelike Characters!

In this comprehensive writing fiction manual, you will learn how to create extraordinary worlds and deeply submerge your readers into the story. Constructing lifelike scenes isn't easy, unless you have the tools to write vibrant, authentic settings.

This manual also provides vital techniques on world-building with bonus examples on how to combine the five senses and use deep POV in all of your scenes. This valuable reference guide is useful in revealing a simplified way to create unique settings and vivid character descriptions flawlessly.

THE WRITER'S GUIDE TO REALISTIC DIALOGUE

A Powerful Reference Tool to Crafting Realistic Conversations in Fiction!

This manual is specifically for fiction writers who want to learn how to create riveting and compelling dialogue that propels the storyline and reveals character personality. Writers will also learn how to weave emotion, description, and action into their dialogue heavy scenes. With a special section on how to instantly improve characterization through gripping conversations. All of these helpful writing tools will make your dialogue sparkle!

THESE BOOKS ARE ON SALE NOW

About the Author

S.A. Soule is a law of attraction enthusiast, who knows a thing or two about manifesting success. Her own fiction and non-fiction publications have graced the Amazon bestseller lists, proving that a little bit of magic (and a whole lot of positivity) can go a long way.

With over two decades of experience and a caffeine-fueled passion for the written word, she's a popular Developmental Editor, Ghostwriter, Published Author, Book Cover Designer, and Plot Consultant/Creator. So, Sherry considers herself a long-time industry veteran.

Her bestselling "Fiction Writing Tools" series offers writers of all levels the tools they need to sharpen their skills and conquer the publishing world. And for those days when writer's block strikes and motivation runs low, her popular "The Positive Writer's Mindset" series is the perfect pick-me-up, providing tips and advice on how to channel your inner author boss and live your best writing life.

When Sherry's not sipping coffee and plotting bookish domination with her feline companions, she can be found curled up with a good book and dreaming up new ways to make procrastination look like a vital part of the creative process.